Gifts
from the
Woodshop

Gifts from the Woodshop

R.J. De Cristoforo

TAB | **TAB BOOKS**
Blue Ridge Summit, PA

FIRST EDITION
FIRST PRINTING

© 1991 by **TAB Books**.
TAB Books is a division of McGraw-Hill, Inc.

Library of Congress Cataloging-in-Publication Data

De Cristoforo, R.J.
    Gifts from the woodshop / by R.J. De Cristoforo.
        p.   cm.
    Includes index.
    ISBN 0-8306-6591   ISBN 0-8306-3591-2 (pbk.)
    1. Woodwork. I. Title.
  TT180.D329 1991
  684′.08—dc20   91-2705
                                                   CIP

TAB Books offers software for sale. For information and a catalog, please contact
TAB Software Department, Blue Ridge Summit, PA 17294-0850.

Acquisitions Editor: Kim Tabor
Book Editor: Susan Rockwell
Production: Katherine G. Brown
Book Design: Jaclyn J. Boone   HT3

Contents

Index   223

Acknowledgment

I owe a special thanks to a person I am sure you are all familiar with—Hank Ketchum, who generously contributed several drawings of his famous "Dennis the Menace." These are contained in the chapter dealing with scroll saw projects.

Introduction

This book is for anyone who has any interest in producing wood projects and who can separate the utilitarian value of the home shop from its therapeutic and enjoyable aspects. It's true—the home workshop can lose its appeal simply because it becomes a workplace used for maintenance and routine chores that are done out of necessity, not choice. A healthy value in production that minimizes if not eliminates the fees of professionals can be made, but if we constantly go from daytime jobs to evening or weekend jobs, then we miss out on the fun aspects of woodworking.

Fun has to do with blanking out the necessary chores and choosing how to spend an evening or weekend. That's why there's the book. All its projects can be produced in a few hours or a day or two. Another, often negative aspect of woodworking, is that a project can seem interminable, even though it's a worthwhile endeavor. Choosing a project or producing one is like brushing aside all constraints and feeling free.

Available tools will have a bearing on production time. It takes more time to saw with a hand tool than with a power tool, but this factor has no bearing on the quality of the output. If, for example, a curved edge is smooth and uniform, it will not be apparent whether the sawing was done with a scroll saw, coping saw, or saber saw. Quality has to do with the intent of the operator.

The word "gifts" should not be taken too literally. Although the projects will be nice offerings for friends or relatives, you can also decide that some particular ones will fill a niche in your home or, when produced in quantity, are viable candidates for a cottage industry with production aimed for placement in a local store, or at county fairs, or at flea markets, or even activities like garage sales.

The reader should not overlook that there is flexibility in terms of "interpreting" the projects. For example, the size of a scroll saw project that is suggested in the drawing does not have to be adhered to strictly. By using larger or smaller squares when transferring a plan, the project can be customized to suit a particular application or space. There is nothing wrong with altering a design element if the change satisfies your esthetic viewpoint.

One of the features of the book is chapter 1—"Shop Data." It contains a considerable amount of material that relates to the shop and woodworking generally. This section can be referred to when making the projects, but as important, it will serve as a standby reference manual for permanent use.

This is a project book and does not pretend to teach the use of tools. It is assumed that the reader already has knowledge in this area and that he or she is aware of essential safety factors. Working carelessly can quickly take the fun out of making things. Always be aware that a tool—hand or power—cannot think for you. It will do your bidding but with disinterest in what you place for it to cut or shape or drill or sand. Whenever you are in doubt about how to approach a particular chore that involves, especially, a power tool, do a dry run first. That is, go through the procedure but with the tool turned off. You can preview how the job will go and judge the safest positions for you and your hands. Remember, "measure twice, cut once," and "think twice before cutting."

Shop Data

In this technological world, there are hordes of invented materials. Although most serve well in the jobs they are designed for, it is not likely that any will take the place of nature's offering—wood. This is especially true in the home workshop since its characteristics make it especially suitable for working with easily available hand or power tools. Power tools can speed up production, but as dedicated hand-tool users know, most constructions can be accomplished successfully using a set of saws, a hammer, and nails. The quality of projects that are produced in a home shop depends on the tool user, not the tools.

Wood (lumber) is classified as "softwood" or "hardwood"—terms that are misunderstood since they are taken literally. Actually, they are botanical designations that distinguish between broad-leaf deciduous trees (hardwood), and evergreens like needle-bearing conifers (softwood). Cedar, redwood, pine, and fir are examples of softwoods; maple, oak, cherry, and birch are typical hardwoods. But, fir, a softwood, is actually "hard"; poplar, a hardwood, is actually "soft."

Lumber

"Lumber" designates wood that has been sawed from a log into usable sizes. Any lumber yard will stock softwood lumber in boards of standard thicknesses and widths and in lengths that increase in increments of 2 feet up to, usually, 20 feet. Technically, lumber has divisions that are based on thickness and width dimensions. A strip is less than 8 inches wide and under 2 inches thick. A board is more than 8 inches wide but less than 2 inches thick. Dimension means 2 inches to 5 inches in thickness and 4 inches to 12 inches in width. The smallest dimension of timber is 6 inches.

Lumber is available as rough, offered without treatment after it has been sawed at the mill. *Milled* means it has been machined into ready-to-use products like siding, flooring, or molding. Dressed (surfaced) is rough material that has been planed so it is ready for use.

The surfacing procedure removes material so the real size of a board is less when you buy it than its nominal size, which is what it measured in the rough. You should ask for lumber in nominal sizes, but as shown in TABLE 1-1, what you will receive has been reduced by planing. For example, if you ask for a $2\times8\times8$, you will receive a piece that measures $1^1/_2$ inches $\times$ $7^1/_4$ inches $\times$ 8 feet. Only the

Table 1-1. Softwood Lumber Sizes (Inches) (Dressed).

	You Ask For	You Receive
	1×2	$^3/_4\times1^1/_2$
	1×3	$^3/_4\times2^1/_2$
	1×4	$^3/_4\times3^1/_2$
	1×6	$^3/_4\times5^1/_2$
	1×8	$^3/_4\times7^1/_4$
	1×10	$^3/_4\times9^1/_4$
	1×12	$^3/_4\times11^1/_4$
	2×2	$1^1/_2\times1^1/_2$
	2×3	$1^1/_2\times2^1/_2$
	2×4	$1^1/_2\times3^1/_2$
	2×6	$1^1/_2\times5^1/_2$
	2×8	$1^1/_2\times7^1/_4$
	2×10	$1^1/_2\times9^1/_4$
	2×12	$1^1/_2\times11^1/_4$
	3×4	$2^1/_2\times3^1/_2$
	4×4	$3^1/_2\times3^1/_2$
	4×6	$3^1/_2\times5^1/_2$

Table 1-1. *Continued.*

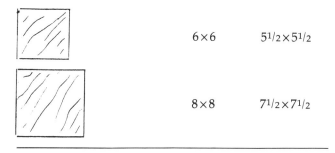

6 × 6	5¹/₂ × 5¹/₂
8 × 8	7¹/₂ × 7¹/₂

length will be what you call for. You can buy a piece that truly measures 1 inch × 4 inches, but it would have to be custom planed from a board of larger dimensions.

Softwood is generally offered in various classifications and grades as noted in TABLE 1-2. These factors should be considered when choosing material for a project, especially since a cost factor is involved. There is little point in paying the price for a material that can be stained or finished naturally if the project will be painted. Often, woodworkers who are making a small project will save by buying material that is less than ideal and culling out the good areas.

Table 1-2. Softwood Lumber Grades.

Grade	Description
Select	
A	Almost perfect material—Does well when stained or finished naturally
B	Like grade "A" but will contain some small defects
C	Will contain defects but they can usually be concealed with paint
D	More defects than "C"—can be concealed with paint
Common	
#1	Utility lumber that is sound and free of checks, splits, or warp—will have tight knots and some blemishes
#2	Reasonably sound but will have end-checks, discoloration and loose knots—should not have warp or splits
#3	Medium-quality construction material—may have all defects—culling out bad parts causes waste
#4	Low quality material with numerous defects including open knotholes
#5	Lowest on the quality chart—pieces can be used as fillers—considerable waste
Structural	
Construction	Top quality for structural applications
Standard	Similar to "construction" but with slight defects
Utility	Poor quality—usually requires strengthening with other structural components
Economy	Very lowest on the quality scale

Hardwood

Hardwood is available in random widths and lengths, and generally, in the thicknesses shown in TABLE 1-3. The surfacing procedure does not reduce thicknesses as drastically as it does on softwood. Although a rough 1 inch piece of softwood is reduced to $3/4$ inch, a similar thickness of hardwood is planed to $13/16$ inch.

Table 1-3. Thicknesses of Hardwood (Inches).

In the Rough (Nominal)	After Surfacing (Two Sides)
$3/8$	$3/16$
$1/2$	$5/16$
$5/8$	$7/16$
$3/4$	$9/16$
1	$13/16$
$1 1/4$	$1 1/16$*
$1 1/2$	$1 5/16$*
2	$1 3/4$
3	$2 3/4$
4	$3 3/4$

* Can be $1/16''$ variation. Hardwood thickness often called out in "quarters," examples—$2/4 = 1/2''$, $5/4 = 1 1/4$.

Hardwood thicknesses are often called out in *quarters*—the quarters being $1/4$ inch. Thus, $5/4$ means $1 1/4$ inch, $3/4$ means $3/4$ inch, and so on.

The National Hardwood Lumber Association has established the grade standards, which are shown in TABLE 1-4, to which producers adhere. The amount of clear or usable area in a board is what determines its grade. Hardwood is expen-

Table 1-4. Hardwood Lumber Grades.

Grade	Description
Firsts	Very fine material for cabinetwork—the wood should be about 92% clear on both surfaces
Seconds	Rivals "firsts" for cabinetwork but needs to be only about 84% clear on both sides
Firsts and seconds	Lumber selection of first two grades but should include at least 20% "firsts"
Selects	One side is not graded but opposite side should be 90% clear—often used for cabinetwork but with some waste expected
#1 Common	Suitable for interior and less demanding cabinetwork—requirement is that it should be about 67% clear on one side
#2 Common	Often selected for paintable work, some wall paneling and flooring—it should be about 50% clear on one side

sive, so be wise when selecting it. Choose less expensive grades for painted projects. A select grade is often fine for cabinetwork since the interior is not visible. Also, check out a cheaper grade when a small project is involved to see if enough "good" material can be culled out.

There are more grades of hardwood than those shown in TABLE 1-4. These are grades that dealers cut apart to remove defects and sell as "shorts," pieces that are narrow in width and short in length. The pieces are often suitable for project components.

Board Foot

The board foot is the accepted unit of lumber measurement. It indicates a piece of wood that has nominal dimensions of 1 inch × 12 feet × 12 inches. As shown in FIG. 1-1, the amount of material, not the shape, determines quantity. A 1-inch-×-6-inch-×-6-foot board equals 3 board feet as does a 1-inch-×-12-inch-×-3-foot board. Some materials are priced and called for by length only (linear foot). These include such items as trim stock, moldings, furring strips, and dowels.

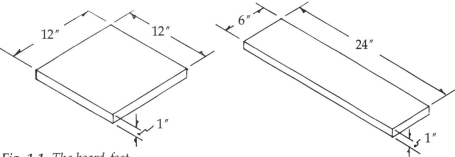

Fig. 1-1. *The board foot.*

A board foot equals a piece that is 1"×12"×12" or its equivalent—to determine board feet, multiply length in feet by thickness and width in inches and divide by 12

$$\underline{\text{Example}} \quad \frac{20' \times 2'' \times 3''}{12} = \frac{120}{12} = 10 \text{ board feet}$$

Plywood

Plywood has many advantages. It is *real* wood that is manufactured into large, usually 4-foot-×-8-foot panels, that have great strength in relation to their weight. Most plywood is made by "peeling" logs on a giant lathe to form veneers of particular thickness that are bonded in odd numbers so the grain direction of one ply is at right angles to the next one. This cross-ply construction provides a strength that solid wood lacks. Wood has strength along the grain but is comparatively weak across the grain. The cross laminations of plywood provide with-the-grain strength in both directions. Another important factor for the woodworker is the size of available panels. Solid wood has width limitations so using it to form a large, quality panel requires time, effort, and expertise.

There are differences in the cores of generally available plywood. The most common type has a core construction that consists of an odd number of veneers, with variations in the number and the thickness of the plies. Lumber, or solid-core plywood has interior material that is much thicker in relation to the surface veneers or to the crossbanding if any is used. The advantage of solid-core has to do with appearance and workability. Often, edges are suitable enough to be exposed, and having a solid edge facilitates installation of hinges or dowels. Veneer-core plywood does not lend itself to such applications, and the edges are seldom pretty enough to be left as-is.

Some of the methods for treating exposed edges of veneer-core plywood are shown in FIG. 1-2. Plain or shaped strips of wood, or suitable moldings can be

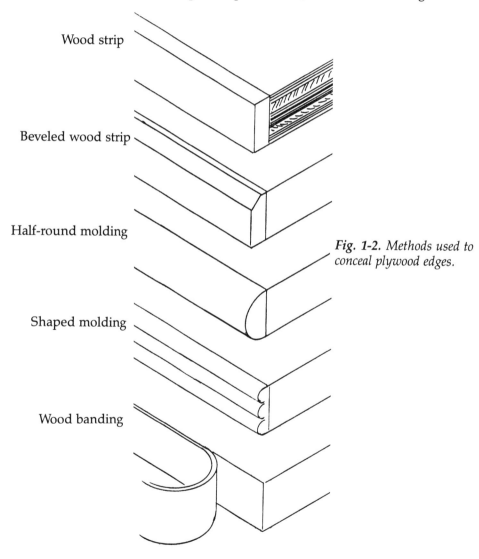

Wood strip

Beveled wood strip

Half-round molding

Fig. 1-2. Methods used to conceal plywood edges.

Shaped molding

Wood banding

glued in place, or adhesive-backed wood banding can be used. The banding, which is thin veneer, is available in many species to match surface veneers and is applied with heat from a household pressing iron. The banding can be applied to any edge but is especially suitable for finishing curved edges.

Grades

Plywood is available for interior or exterior use and in the categories that are listed in TABLE 1-5. All panels are, or should be, stamped to reveal the construction. Softwood plywood, which can have surface veneers of Douglas fir, pine, redwood, and numerous other wood species, is suitable for applications that

Table 1-5. Grades of Plywood.

| Grade | Veneer Quality | | | Applications |
	Face	Back	Plies	
Exterior				
A-A	A	A	C	When the project requires a good appearance on both sides—good for signs, fences, furniture
A-B	A	B	C	A good substitute for A-A if the appearance of the project on one side is not important
A-C	A	C	C	Has one good side—good for structural applications, fences, outbuildings
B-C	B	C	C	Utility projects—out buildings, some fences, a base for other coatings
Siding 303	C	C	C	Variety of surface textures and groove patterns—good for fences, screens, unique touches on projects
MDO	B	B-C	C	(Medium density overlay) built-ins, signs, excellent base for paint
Interior				
A-A	A	A	D	Doors for cabinetry, built-ins, projects where both sides of the material will show
A-B	A	B	D	Can be substituted for A-A when back surface is not important
A-D	A	D	D	Face is finish grade—use for paneling, built-ins, backing for projects
B-D	B	D	D	Utility grade—okay for backing, cabinet sides, etc.
C-D	C	D	D	Structural uses and sheathing—unsanded—often used for subflooring

span from house construction to interior cabinet work and small projects. An important element, in relation to the proposed project, is the choice of surface veneer. These also adhere to a standard grade program as listed in TABLE 1-6.

Hardwood plywood is superior material with surface veneers that can range from mahogany, walnut, oak, and other familiar woods to the most exotic of

Table 1-6. Plywood Veneer Grades.

Grade	Description
A	Smooth surfaces—paintable—neat repairs are allowed—will take a natural finish on less demanding projects
B	Tight knots and circular repair plugs are allowed
C	Larger knotholes allowed (1″ to 1$\frac{1}{2}$″)—total area of blemishes limited by industry standards—some splits allowed
C (Plugged)	Improved "C" veneer—width of splits limited to $\frac{1}{8}$″—knotholes and other blemishes can't be more than $\frac{1}{4}$″ × $\frac{1}{2}$″
D	Limited number of splits allowed—knots and knotholes can be as large as 2$\frac{1}{2}$″

imported species. Grades are established so the appearance and the quality can be judged; #1—custom grade, is free of defects but the surface, so long as color and grain are carefully matched, can be more than one piece; #2 departs from the custom grade in that matching is not considered overly critical; #3 is suitable for a painted project but a clear finish is not advisable since some blemishes like streaks or stains are allowed; #4, a utility grade, will have knots and might show discoloration; #5, often referred to as a backing grade, has negative appearance elements such as large knots and even splits. The grading can apply to one or both surfaces of a panel.

Unusual Surfaces

Plywood panels with textured surfaces, like those shown in FIGS. 1-3 and 1-4, can be used to add decorative touches to many projects. Although they are meant to be used as wall coverings usually, there is no reason why they cannot be used for

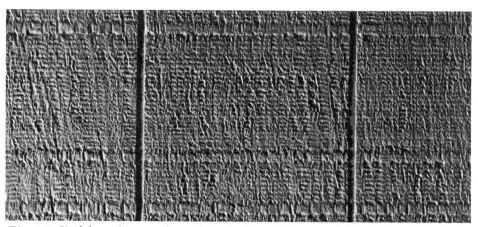

Fig. 1-3. Kerfed rough-sawn plywood is actually a siding material but it is suitable for in-the-shop projects.

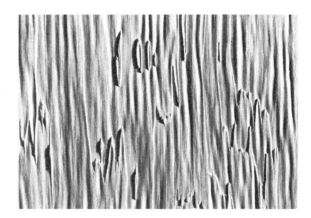

Fig. 1-4. Brushed plywood has interesting surface texture. Like kerfed rough-sawn, it is exterior grade and is a nice choice for plant containers.

small projects in or outside of the house. A plant container, for example, will be more interesting if its surfaces have a texture.

Another product of interest to the woodworker is *medium density overlaid* (MDO). The surface of the softwood plywood is baked-on phenolic resin. Although the material is intended for use as a house siding, its exceptional paint-ability makes it suitable for in-the-shop projects.

Fasteners

The variety in nails is impressive. The ones in FIG. 1-5 are a selection of types that are frequently used on in-the-shop projects. Common and box nails are similar; the latter being the slimmer of the two and chosen when a heavier nail might

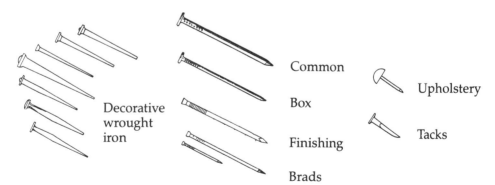

Decorative wrought iron

Common

Box

Finishing

Brads

Upholstery

Tacks

Fig. 1-5. Nail types. Wrought iron nails can be purchased through catalogs. They can add decorative touches to many projects.

cause splitting. Nails are sized by the *penny* (d) system, which once indicated cost but now tells the length of the nail (TABLE 1-7). A common rule for nail length is to choose one that is three times longer than the thickness of the piece being secured (the face piece), but the rule is often broken. You would not use a 1½

Table 1-7. Common Nails.

Penny (d) Size	Length (11 in.)	Wire Gauge
2	1	15
3	$1^{1}/4$	14
4	$1^{1}/2$	$12^{1}/2$
5	$1^{3}/4$	$12^{1}/2$
6	2	$11^{1}/2$
7	$2^{1}/4$	$11^{1}/4$
8	$2^{1}/2$	$10^{1}/4$
9	$2^{3}/4$	$10^{1}/4$
10	3	9
12	$3^{1}/4$	9
16	$3^{1}/2$	8
20	4	6
30	$4^{1}/2$	5
40	5	4
50	$5^{1}/2$	3
60	6	2

Box nails are slimmer than common nails but come in same lengths.

inch (4d) nail to join two pieces of $1/2$-inch stock. In such cases, the nail should be long enough for security without passing through.

Casing and finishing nails (TABLE 1-8) differ from common and box types in

Table 1-8. Finishing Nails and Casing Nails.

Penny (d) Size	Length (11 in.)	Gauge
Finishing	1	$16^{1}/2$
2	1	$15^{1}/2$
3	$1^{1}/4$	$15^{1}/2$
4	$1^{1}/2$	15
5	$1^{1}/4$	15
6	2	13
8	$2^{1}/2$	$12^{1}/2$
10	3	$11^{1}/2$
16	$3^{1}/2$	11
20	4	10
Casing		
3	$1^{1}/4$	$14^{1}/2$
4	$1^{1}/2$	14
6	2	$12^{1}/2$
8	$2^{1}/2$	$11^{1}/2$
10	3	$10^{1}/2$
16	$3^{1}/2$	10

that they are designed to be hidden. They are driven almost flush with the surface and driven additionally to about $1/16$ inch below the surface by using a nail set. The hole is then filled with a wood dough. A trick used by many professionals is to first use a sharp knife or chisel to lift a sliver of wood. The nail is driven in the depression and the sliver is glued back. When this is done carefully, it is not possible to tell that a nail was used.

Nails are available in a variety of materials, the most common being mild steel. These are fine for most applications but if the project will be exposed to weather or dampness, use galvanized nails or those made of a rust-proof material like aluminum.

Brads and tacks (TABLE 1-9) are used for light-duty fastening. Although the sizes of tacks are designated by numbers, brads are usually identified by actual length. Brads, like finishing nails, are usually set below the surface of the wood and hidden with wood dough.

Corrugated nails and *skotch* fasteners, shown in FIG. 1-6, are special fasteners that have particular applications. Corrugated nails are ribbed lengths of metal that are sharpened along one edge. Generally, they are used when appearance is not important, or when they are hidden. These should be used across the grain; driving them with the grain can cause splitting. *Skotch* nails used in similar applications, are less "hazardous" than corrugated nails since they penetrate the wood with individual prongs so there is less chance of splitting.

Table 1-9. Tacks and Brads

	Part No.	Length (Inches)
Tacks	2	$1/4$
	$2^{1}/2$	$5/16$
	3	$3/8$
	4	$7/16$
	6	$1/2$
	8	$9/16$
	10	$5/8$
	12	$11/16$
	14	$3/4$
	16	$13/16$
	18	$7/8$
	22	1

	Length (Inches)	Gauge
Brads	$3/16$	20 – 24
	$1/4$	19 – 24
	$3/8$	18 – 24
	$1/2$	14 – 23
	$5/8$	13 – 22
	$3/4$	13 – 21
	$7/8$	13 – 20

Corrugated nails

Fig. 1-6. Different ''nails'' that can be used on rough assemblies or in hidden areas.

"Scotch" nails

Nailing Hints

In essence, a nail holds because wood fibers tend to return to original positions, thus gripping the shank of the nail. That is why the carnival trick of driving a nail with a minimum number of blows is not wise. Powerful blows will distort or break fibers so they will not grip as well as they should.

You can sometimes save a nail that bends by straightening it at the bend with a pair of pliers, but it is best to remove the nail and discard it. Do not drive many nails on a common centerline especially with the grain since splitting is likely. Did you ever see a professional carpenter blunt a nail point with a slight tap of the hammer? He does it because a slightly blunt point is less likely to cause splitting than a sharp one.

Do not hesitate to drill a pilot hole for nails if there is a splitting potential or the wood is very hard. Some workers will remove the head from a nail and use it like a drill bit. This will cause more burning than drilling but it is a usable technique to form limited-depth starting holes.

Screws

Screws cost more than nails and it takes a little more time and know-how to seat them but special characteristics make them ideal for many projects. They can hold more securely than nails, and they can be more decorative. On projects in which the fastener will be exposed, a round head or oval head screw is often more acceptable than a nail head. Also, screws are removable so a component can be removed or an entire project can be broken down.

Common screws and the types of washers that can be used with them are shown in FIG. 1-7. Screws are identified by number and length. The number will specify the shank diameter but the length required for the project is needed. Pertinent information is offered in TABLE 1-10.

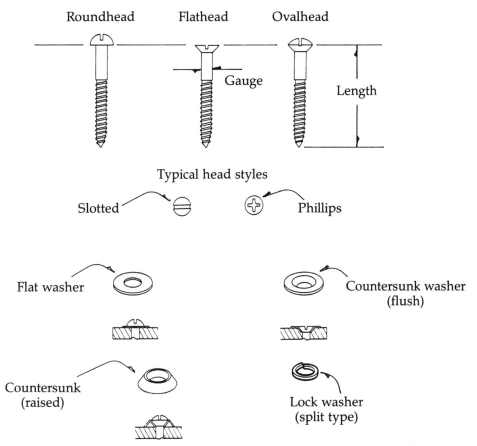

Roundhead   Flathead   Ovalhead

Gauge

Length

Typical head styles

Slotted   Phillips

Flat washer   Countersunk washer
                     (flush)

Countersunk   Lock washer
(raised)   (split type)

Fig. 1-7. Common woodscrews and washers that can be used with them. Washers add bearing surface and increase the gripping power of the screw.

A special drilling procedure is required for screws to drive easily and to hold with maximum strength. Tapping them with a hammer and forcing them into the wood will not work. You will have two types of holes: a body hole that suits the shank diameter, and a pilot hole that, technically, is suitable for the root diameter of the threaded portion (FIG. 1-8 and TABLE 1-11). Both of the needed holes can be formed with drill bits; however, special screw-hole formers that do the whole job precisely make the chore easier and faster. The cutters are available in sizes for most screws and some are designed to provide a countersink or a counterbore or both. A countersink is needed so flathead screws can be driven flush with surfaces, a counterbore is used when a screw is driven below the surface of the wood so it can be hidden with a plain plug or a decorative button.

The more thread there is in the wood, the better the screw will hold. The longest screw that is suitable for the job should be selected. The common rule

Table 1-10.

Real Shank Size	# of Screws	Shank Diameter	Commonly Available Lengths
	2	.086	$1/4-1/2''$
	3	.099	$1/4-5/8''$
	4	.112	
			$3/8-3/4''$
	5	.125	
	6	.138	
			$3/8''-1^1/2''$
	7	.151	
	8	.164	$1/2''-2''$
	9	.177	$5/8''-2^1/4''$
	10	.190	
	12	.216	$7/8''-2^1/2''$
	14	.242	$1''-2^3/4''$
	16	.268	$1^1/4''-3''$
	18	.294	$1^1/2''-4''$
	20	.320	$1^3/4''-4''$
	24	.372	$3^1/2''-4''$

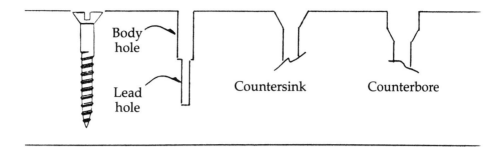

Body hole

Lead hole

Countersink

Counterbore

Screws can be concealed with plugs
sanded flush or with decorative
buttons

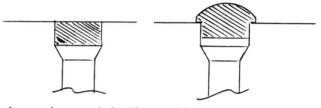

Fig. 1-8. Nomenclature of a screw hole. Plugs and buttons are available in various sizes.

Table 1-11. Drill Sizes for Flathead Wood Screws.

Size of Screw	Body Hole Fractional Size	Body Hole No. or Letter	Lead Hole Hardwood Fractional Size	Lead Hole Hardwood No. or Letter	Lead Hole Softwood Fractional Size	Lead Hole Softwood No. or Letter
0	1/16	52	1/32	70	—	—
1	5/64	47	1/32	66	1/32	71
2	3/32	42	3/64	56	1/32	65
3	7/64	37	1/16	54	3/64	58
4	7/64	32	1/16	52	3/64	55
5	1/8	30	5/64	49	1/16	53
6	9/64	27	5/64	47	1/16	52
7	5/32	22	3/32	44	1/16	51
8	11/64	18	3/32	40	5/64	48
9	3/16	14	7/64	37	5/64	45
10	3/16	10	7/64	33	3/32	43
11	13/64	4	1/8	31	3/32	40
12	7/32	2	1/8	30	7/64	38
14	1/4	D	9/64	25	7/64	32
16	17/64	I	5/32	18	9/64	29
18	19/64	N	3/16	13	9/64	26
20	21/64	P	13/64	4	11/64	19
24	3/8	V	7/32	1	3/16	15

Fractional drill sizes are close—letter and number sizes are more accurate.

says that the screw length should be about $1/8$ inch less than the combined thickness of the components. To secure two pieces of $3/4$-inch stock, you should choose a screw that is $1^3/8$ inches in length.

Heavy-Duty Fasteners

Heavy-duty fasteners, like those shown in FIG. 1-9, do a good job when projects involve heavy materials or are subjected to a lot of stress. Lag screws are driven much like ordinary screws but with a wrench or sockets. Machine bolts and carriage bolts require a hole through both parts. An advantage of the carriage bolt is the way its head is formed. The tapered shoulders under the dome sink into the wood and keep the bolt from turning. Thus, it can be secured with a single wrench on the nut.

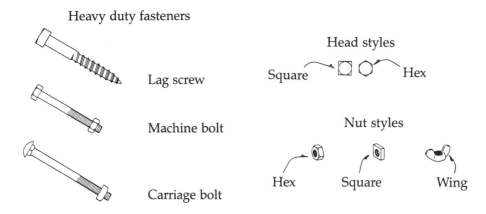

Fig. 1-9. Heavy-duty fasteners. Wing nuts can be used on machine or carriage bolts.

Special Inserts

Threaded inserts and *T-nuts* (FIG. 1-10) make it possible to install metal threads in wood. The T-nut, which is visible, has prongs that sink into the wood when it is

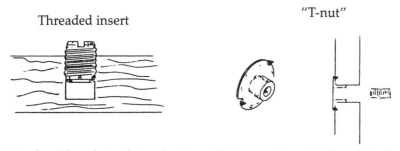

Fig. 1-10. Special products that make it possible to provide metal threads in lumber or plywood.

tapped into a suitable hole. The inserts have exterior threads and can be driven in blind holes so they will not be visible. Both items are available in various sizes and can be used for light or heavy-duty applications.

Reinforcements

Metal plates that are available in many shapes and sizes can add considerable strength to a variety of woodworking connections (FIG. 1-11). Most times they are used in hidden areas but many people have used them creatively, leaving them exposed and painted black, to add a decorative wrought-iron touch to a project.

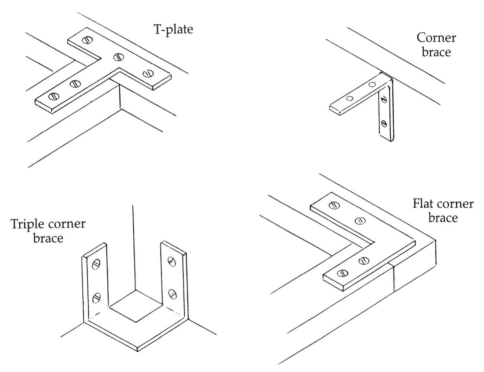

Fig. 1-11. Various types of reinforcement products. They can be painted black to resemble wrought iron.

Abrasives

You can spend a lot of time and do a good job constructing a project and ruin it by being lax with the last step—wood smoothing, which should take place before the application of stain or paint or clear finish. Dedication in this area varies but no options are available. Sanding can be the difference between a professional looking project and an amateurish one, and it doesn't matter whether you are sanding by hand or with a power tool.

Table 1-12. Basic Information About Abrasives.

Name	Available Grits	Sizes	For Wood	Metal	Typical Uses
Flint	Very fine to very coarse	9″×10″ 4¹/₂″×5″	X		Rough work—used for finishing chores but lacks toughness and durability
Garnet	220–30	9″×11″	X		Very good for general woodworking applications
Aluminum oxide	220–30	9″×11″	X	X	Long lasting—good for hardwoods—may be used on non-wood materials
Aluminum oxide (cloth)	120–30	Belt form for electric sanders	X	X	Cloth-backed belts are very strong and are a number one choice for power sanding
Silicon carbide (waterproof)	400–220	9″×11″	X	X	Excellent for sanding after primer coats and between finish coats—often used with water and other lubricants

Many abrasives are available in sizes that are just right for power tools like pad sanders—some modern abrasives have self-adhesive backing for pad and disc sanders.

Table 1-13. Sandpaper Grits.

Degree	Grit No.	Grade No.	Typical Uses
Very fine	400	10/0	Super-fine surface on raw wood—use after applying stain, shellac, sealers—polishing and smoothing between finish coats and for smoothing of the final coat
	360	—	
	320	9/0	
	280	8/0	
	240	7/0	
	220	6/0	
Fine	180	5/0	Can be used for finishing raw wood before applications of stains and sealers
	150	4/0	
	120	3/0	
Medium	100	2/0	Intermediate smoothing—preparing surfaces for final work with fine paper
	80	1/0	
	60	1/2	
Coarse	50	1	Use when necessary, for first sanding to prepare wood for final work with finer abrasive
	40	1¹/₂	
	36	2	
Very Coarse	30	2¹/₂	For very rough work only—use on wood in-the-rough—often used in place of a file or plane to round edges
	24	3	
	20	3¹/₂	
	16	4	

Information regarding types of abrasives and the grits they are available in is offered in TABLES 1-12 and 1-13. At one time, flint was widely used but it has taken a back seat to harder, longer lasting materials like garnet and aluminum oxide.

Sandpaper is a cutting tool. It removes wood by various degrees in relation to the coarseness of the abrasive. The general rule is to work through progressively finer grits until the wood feels satiny smooth, but automatically choosing a coarse grit to begin with is not always the best way to go. Since most of the wood and wood products we work with today are in fairly good shape to begin with, the optimum finish can be achieved by starting with a medium paper or even a fine paper. Sawed edges, especially on plywood will, of course, require more attention than surfaces.

The terms *open-coat* and *close-coat* reveal how much of the backing is covered with the abrasive grit. Close-coat has overall coverage and will produce the smoothest finish. Open-coat has 50 to 70% coverage and resists clogging, which is why it is the choice for working on old wood and for removing finishes. It is also a good choice for resinous wood.

For smoothest results, final sanding is done with the grain. You can work cross-grain when you want to remove a lot of material quickly but the scratches that result must be eliminated by final sanding that is parallel to the grain of the wood.

Adhesives

Durable joints that are stronger than the wood itself are the result when the best glue is selected and applied with care. There are many wood-bonding products that are available today and they all have impressive gripping power, but a good choice depends on the characteristics of the glue and the nature of the work. The most available adhesives and their features and typical applications are listed in TABLE 1-14.

Surfaces to be joined should be clean, dry, and smooth. It pays to do a test assembly to be sure that parts will mate as they should before you apply the glue. Being too generous with the glue is a common error. There should be a minimum of squeeze-out when the pieces are clamped or fastened. This is economical and reduces the cleaning chore of removing the excess. The best way to remove the extra is with a sharp chisel while the glue is still soft; use a cloth dampened (not soaked) with warm water to finish.

Extra glue on surfaces must be removed or it will act like a sealer, preventing finishes from penetrating or showing through them. Sanding can be done to get rid of extra glue but do not sand if the glue is still wet; you will only force the adhesive deeper into the wood.

Endgrain and plywood edges are absorbent so they require more glue. Apply a second coat after the first one has had a chance to settle.

Table 1-14. Common Adhesives.

Name	To Prepare	Moisture Resistance	Waterproof	Applications
Liquid hide	Ready to use	Good	No	Easy to use—resist heat—okay for general furniture work but not for outdoor projects
Casein	Water mix	Good	No	Very good for oily woods like teak and yew—will stain species like redwood—okay for general woodworking
Polyvinyl	Ready to use	Good	No	Quick settings, easy to use, and needs minimum clamping time—good choice for general woodworking
Plastic resin	Water mix	High	No	Not good for oily woods—good for projects that will be exposed to considerable moisture
Resorcinol	2-part mix	Very high	Yes	The glue to use for outdoor projects—best used at temperatures 70°F or higher
Contact cement	Ready to use	High	No	Not for general woodworking—generally used for bonding thin materials like laminates and veneers to a sub-structure—bonds on contact
Epoxy cement	2-part mix	Very high	Yes	Not for general woodworking—good for bonding dissimilar materials—some types can be used to fill holes—must be used very carefully
Hot melt (sticks)	Used with heat gun	Good	Some yes	Not for general woodworking—various types of adhesive sticks available for gluing, caulking, bonding dissimilar materials—good for temporary spot-gluing

Clamping time, mixing procedure when needed, and best temperature to use at, vary. Always study the instructions on the container before using the product.

Readymades

By *readymades*, we mean commercial products that are ready to use as project components (FIG. 1-12). Some, like dowel pegs, have a utilitarian purpose, being designed for use in, for example, edge-to-edge joints. Others, like axles, wheels, candle cups, and such, are ready to install, thereby saving time and effort. Items of this nature can be purchased individually but they are often offered as assortments that might even include storage bins (FIG. 1-13). Most craftsman and tool catalogs list an assortment of readymades.

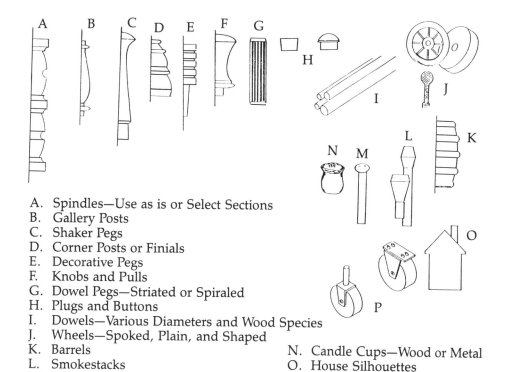

A. Spindles—Use as is or Select Sections
B. Gallery Posts
C. Shaker Pegs
D. Corner Posts or Finials
E. Decorative Pegs
F. Knobs and Pulls
G. Dowel Pegs—Striated or Spiraled
H. Plugs and Buttons
I. Dowels—Various Diameters and Wood Species
J. Wheels—Spoked, Plain, and Shaped
K. Barrels
L. Smokestacks
M. Axles

N. Candle Cups—Wood or Metal
O. House Silhouettes
P. Casters—Swivel or Plate

Fig. 1-12. Typical readymades.

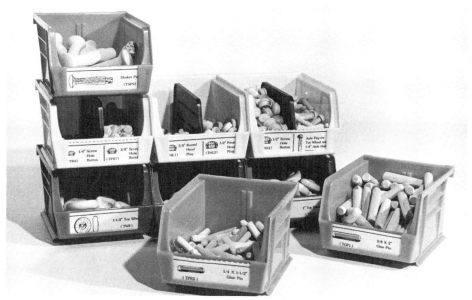

Fig. 1-13. Assortments of readymades are offered in many craftsman catalogs.

Shop Tips

Folks who work with power tools will rely on a machine to form joint components like dadoes and rabbets but hand-tool operators can do as well. It just takes a bit more time. To form a dado, which is simply a U-shaped groove, use a back saw or a dovetail saw, as shown in FIG. 1-14, to make the shoulder cuts. A strip of wood, clamped to the saw, will control the depth of the cuts. Remove the waste by working carefully with a sharp chisel (FIG. 1-15). Make additional saw cuts between the first ones and the last step will be easier.

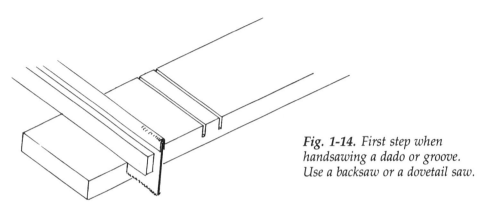

Fig. 1-14. First step when handsawing a dado or groove. Use a backsaw or a dovetail saw.

Fig. 1-15. The waste between the shoulder cuts is removed with a chisel.

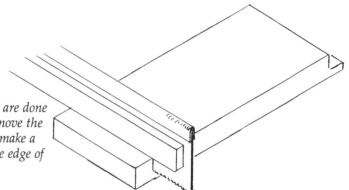

Fig. 1-16. Rabbet cuts are done in similar fashion. Remove the waste with a chisel or make a second saw cut into the edge of the stock.

A rabbet, which is an L-shaped cut on the end or edge of stock, is formed in similar fashion, the difference being that you make a single shoulder cut (FIG. 1-16). The waste can be removed with a chisel or with a second saw cut into the edge of the material.

Angular cuts can be done freehand but accuracy will be easier to achieve by working with a miter box (FIG. 1-17). This type of accessory can be purchased but it is better to make your own so it will be right for the saw you plan to use. Plans for one that has a ledge so it can be gripped in a vise are offered in FIG. 1-18. The design calls for guide-slots at 45 and 90 degrees but you can add others if a cut calls for a different angle. This should not be overdone since too many slots will

Fig. 1-17. A miter box makes it easy to saw angular cuts accurately. The accessory should be used with a backsaw.

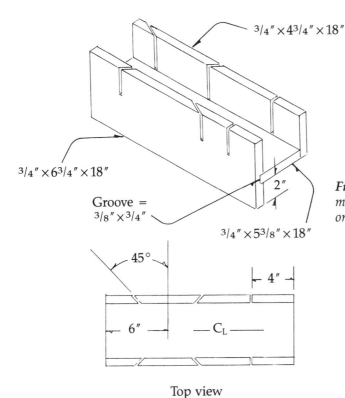

$3/4'' \times 4 3/4'' \times 18''$

$3/4'' \times 6 3/4'' \times 18''$

Groove = $3/8'' \times 3/4''$

2''

$3/4'' \times 5 3/8'' \times 18''$

Fig. 1-18. *Construction details of a miter box that can be used for square or 45-degree cuts.*

45°

4''

6''

C_L

Top view

weaken the project. If necessary, make a second miter box to accommodate odd angles.

Drilling holes at right angles to a surface or an edge can be tricky when attempted freehand. A better way is to prepare a guide block like the one shown in FIG. 1-19. Mark its edges with centerlines so it can be aligned with intersecting lines that are marked on the workpiece. The guide should have a small hole since it will be used to locate pilot holes in the work. The pilot holes can be enlarged to the size that is needed.

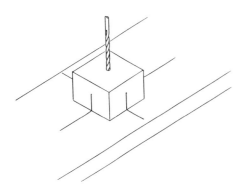

Fig. 1-19. *A drill guide will ensure that holes will be perpendicular to surfaces.*

Figure 1-20 shows a similar accessory that can be used for drilling holes into stock edges. This type should be made to accommodate the thickness of the stock that is being worked on.

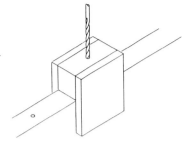

Fig. 1-20. *Drill guides can also be made for drilling into the edges of stock.*

Child's Play

There is a vicarious pleasure in making projects for children. In addition to the fun of making them, there is the anticipation of giving them and watching the receiver's enjoyment. Someplace in there is the scenario of our own young days. Toy production can take an altruistic form. Even if there are not any children in the immediate scene, many agencies are prepared to receive them for needy children.

Many commercial toys are made of plastic but in the home shop, wood is the traditional material. Lumber and plywood are the mainstays, and they are readily available. Since toy projects do not require a lot of material, lumber and plywood are economical to use. Whether to use a softwood like pine or a hardwood like maple is often arbitrary even though the purpose of some projects or components might suggest a choice. Wheels, for example, must endure, so they should be made with maple or birch. A child's chair should be made with a cabinet grade material like lumber core plywood.

Children do not object to playthings with a natural finish, so sand well and end with a protective, clear coating. Painting, of course, is the way to go when color is important. Check containers to ensure that the contents are nontoxic, and safe for youngsters to play with.

Bassinet

There are many sophisticated, grown-up dolls with extensive wardrobes for partying but our bassinet (FIG. 2-1) is for the baby doll. Start the project by studying the construction details in FIG. 2-2. Hold the sides together with double-face tape or by tacknailing two 3/8-inch-×-11½-inch-×-18-inch pieces of cabinet-grade

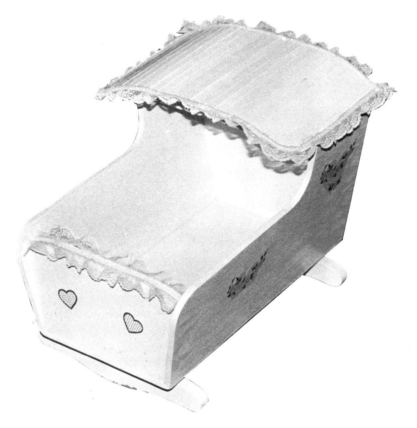

Fig. 2-1. Bassinet is trimmed with readymade lace and decorated with self adhesive decals.

plywood so the good faces are outward. Mark the outline on one side and saw the pieces to shape. Cut the back to size, curving the top to the form that is shown in FIG. 2-3A. Cut the front and the forward canopy support to overall size and since top edges on all three pieces are similar, use the back as a pattern to mark the others. Assemble the sides, front, and back with glue and 1-inch brads.

Place the assembly on a piece of 3/8-inch plywood and trace around it for the shape of the bottom. Add the bottom to the assembly, again using glue and 1-inch brads, and wrap a piece of sandpaper around a wood block and use it to smooth the perimeter of the bottom to match the slant of the sides. Next, add the front canopy support with glue and two nails at each end. Be sure the top edges of the support and the back are on the same plane.

Shape the rocker feet by following the plan that is shown in FIG. 2-3B. The rockers can be sawed individually with a coping saw but if you work with a scroll

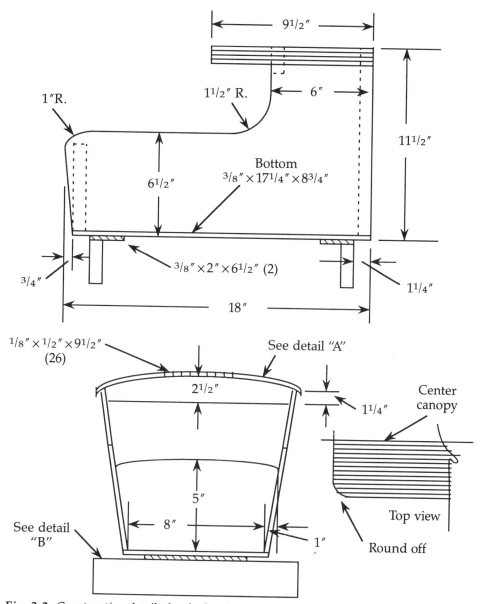

Fig. 2-2. *Construction details for the bassinet.*

saw or bandsaw you can save time and effort by putting two pieces of stock together as a pad and sawing them as if they were a solid block.

Attach the rockers to the small pads and put the subassemblies in place by using glue and driving two or three 4d box nails through the bottom of the bassinet into the legs.

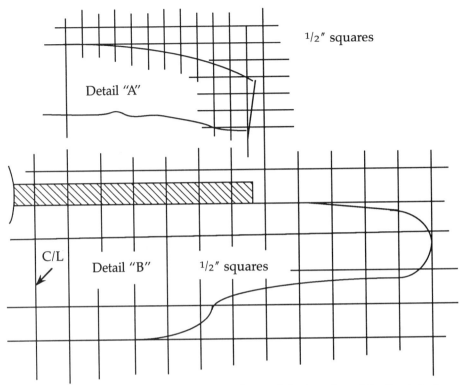

Fig. 2-3. *Contour details for the bassinet's rockers and the top edges of the front, back, and canopy support.*

The canopy consists of strips of $1/8$-inch-$\times$-$1/2$-inch plywood that are secured with glue and a single $1/2$-inch brad at each end. Start installation at a center point and work out toward each side. Round off the front corners after the glue has set. A flexible material can be used instead of slats for the canopy; heavy, smooth-surfaced art board or a plastic laminate might do. If you decide on an option, be sure the material will not have sharp edges.

Sand all surfaces, giving edges particular attention. Wrap sandpaper around a block of wood and stroke corners so they will be slightly rounded. A good finish consists of a first coat of sanding sealer that you smooth when dry, and then two coats of paint. Trim the canopy and the top edge of the front with a lace fringe. The material is available ready-to-use from shops that supply knitting goods and can be attached with an adhesive that works on porous surfaces. The final step is to add decorative touches by using colorful decals. Many types of self adhesive decals are available with designs ranging from cartoon characters to delicate florals.

Child's Seat

Children seem to acquire an adult air and they feel more important when they are presented with furniture that is exclusively their own. A seat, or chair if you prefer, seems a logical first project in this area. The one shown in FIG. 2-4 employs a clean design and can be made from less than a half sheet of plywood. A lumber core, maple, or birch plywood with good veneer on both surfaces is recommended.

Fig. 2-4. Child's seat. A project like this deserves a good, cabinet-grade, hardwood plywood.

Start by cutting two pieces 12 inches × 14 inches. Whether surface grain should run vertically or horizontally is optional. Mark the side profile on one piece (FIG. 2-5), and pad the two pieces by driving nails into waste areas. Sawing will be easier if you mark the meeting point of cuts and bore holes to form the round corners. The job can be finished with mostly straight cuts.

Mark the locations of parts 4 and 5 (cleats) on the inside faces of the sides. Make the cleats of hardwood and attach them with glue and three #12, 1¼-inch flat-head wood screws through each of them. Be sure to countersink carefully so the screw heads will be flush.

Prepare the seat and back and put the parts together temporarily to be sure that everything meshes. The back is installed with glue and three #12, 1½-inch flat-head wood screws into each cleat. If you have bar clamps, use them to hold the parts snugly together while you do the installation. It is also a good idea to have the seat in place so the sides and back will be square to each other.

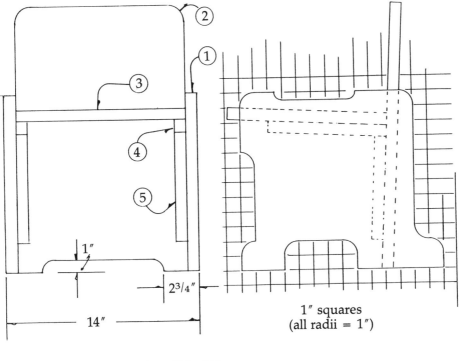

1″

2³/4″

14″

1″ squares
(all radii = 1″)

2 #1—³/4″ × 12″ × 14″
1 #2—³/4″ × 12¹/2″ × 18″
1 #3—³/4″ × 11″ × 12¹/2″
2 #4—³/4″ × 1¹/2″ × 8″
2 #5—³/4″ × 1¹/2″ × 7″
Use cabinet grade plywood

Fig. 2-5. The plan for the child's seat. All assembling is done with glue and screws.

The final step is to glue and screw the seat in place. There is a choice here. You can use oval-head screws with countersunk washers, or flat-head screws that you drive about ¹/8 inch below the surface of the wood and conceal with wood plugs. In either case, use #12 screws, 1¹/2 inches long.

Since the project is made of a fancy plywood, a clear finish should be used. One way to go is to first apply a coat of sanding sealer. Go over all surfaces with fine sandpaper after the sealer is dry. Use a tack cloth or any lintfree cloth to remove all dust and apply a second coat of sealer, followed by another sanding. A heavy coat of paste wax, rubbed to a polish can complete the job or you can end with a final coat of something like a polyurethane varnish. If you use varnish, sand lightly after it is thoroughly dry, and polish with wax. Pay special attention to edges since they will absorb more finish than surfaces. Many times, it pays to coat edges and allow them to dry before proceeding with overall coverage.

Toy-Tote Wagon

The project shown in FIG. 2-6 can be used indoors for a child to store or tote toys about or as an outdoor plaything. This might suggest the material to use—hardwood plywood for the main components for indoors, or a respectable grade of fir plywood for rougher outside use. Actually, you could use solid lumber since the sizes of the components are not that extreme.

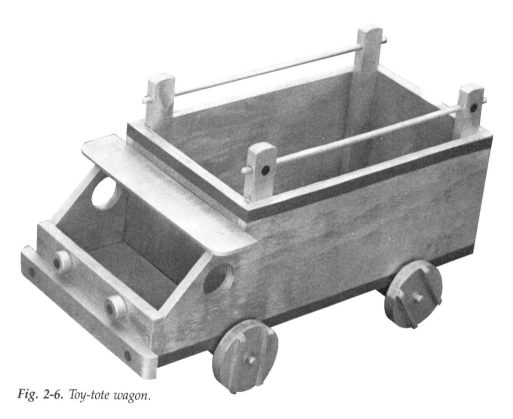

Fig. 2-6. Toy-tote wagon.

All construction details are contained in FIG. 2-7. Start by sizing two pieces ³/4 inch × 8 inches × 24 inches for the sides and tacknailing them together so they can be shaped simultaneously. The only cuts required are for the slant of the cab area and the notch for the roof of the cab. Bore the 2-inch diameter hole while the pieces are still joined.

Two pieces, ³/4 inch × 8 inches × 10 inches, form the back of the wagon and the rear of the cab area. Install them with glue and 6d finishing nails. Next, form the four ³/4-inch-×-1¹/2-inch-×-11-inch corner posts. Round off the top edges and drill through them for the ³/8-inch dowel before you install them by using glue and 4d box nails. The posts add detail, but they also add considerable strength to the assembly.

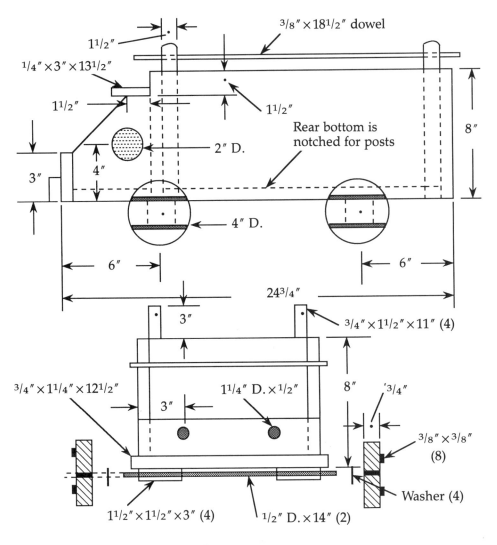

Toy-tote wagon

Fig. 2-7. *How the toy-tote wagon is put together.*

The bottom of the project is composed of two pieces. The rear one is notched at the corners to accommodate the posts; the front one has square corners and is the base of the cab area. Both are secured with glue and 6d finishing nails. Make and install the front and top of the cab and add the bumper. The headlights are 1/2-inch thick slices of large dowel, attached with glue and a single 3d finishing nail. Drill a small pilot hole before driving the nail to avoid the possibility of splitting the dowel.

Make the axle blocks and drill a 9/16-inch hole through them. The holes are oversized so the axles can turn freely. Mark the location of the blocks on the underside of the project and install them with glue and 7d box nails. Drill pilot holes for the nails, being sure to locate them so they don't pass through the axle holes. If you put the axles in place as you attach the blocks, you can be sure of alignment.

The 3/4-inch-thick, hardwood wheels are 4 inches in diameter. They are not difficult to make if you have a drill press and a fly cutter. You can, of course, substitute commercial ones even if they are a bit larger or smaller. The cross pieces on the wheels are optional but they add some sturdiness even if it is only visual. Attach them with glue and 3/4-inch brads. The axles fit loosely in the blocks but are a tight fit in the wheels. It does not hurt to use glue when you press the wheels onto the axles.

Set all nailheads below the surface of the wood and conceal them by using a wood dough. Sand well, paying particular attention to edges and corners and finish. The project in this book is silver, and decorated with strips of contrasting, self-adhesive tape.

Biplane

The biplane (FIG. 2-8) does not come close to being an SST but kids can roll it like the Red Baron or simply display it. Figure 2-9 shows how the components go

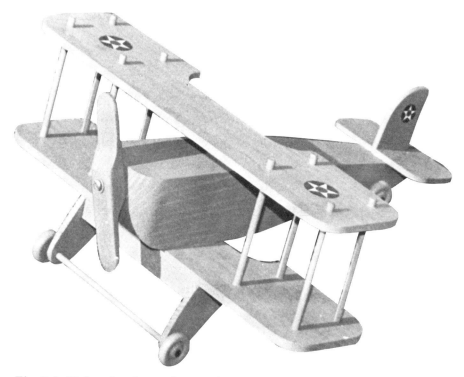

Fig. 2-8. Biplane is a far cry from modern aircraft but that doesn't seem to bother youngsters.

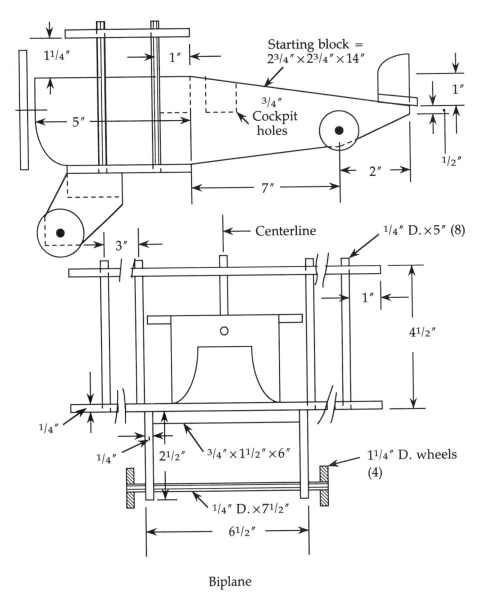

Starting block =
$2^3/4'' \times 2^3/4'' \times 14''$

$1^1/4''$

$1''$

$3/4''$
Cockpit
holes

$5''$

$1''$

$1/2''$

$2''$

$7''$

Centerline

$1/4''$ D. $\times 5''$ (8)

$3''$

$1''$

$4^1/2''$

$1/4''$

$1/4''$

$2^1/2''$

$3/4'' \times 1^1/2'' \times 6''$

$1^1/4''$ D. wheels
(4)

$1/4''$ D. $\times 7^1/2''$

$6^1/2''$

Biplane

Fig. 2-9. *Assembly of the biplane.*

together, whereas FIG. 2-10 offers details for most of the parts.

The fuselage is a $2^3/4$-inch square $\times$ 14-inch block of softwood. Bore the cock-pit holes and the hole for the rear axle before you do any shaping. Forming the contours will be easy if you can work with a bandsaw, otherwise do the major cutting with a handsaw and the shaping of the front end with a rasp. Smooth all saw cuts and rasped areas with sandpaper.

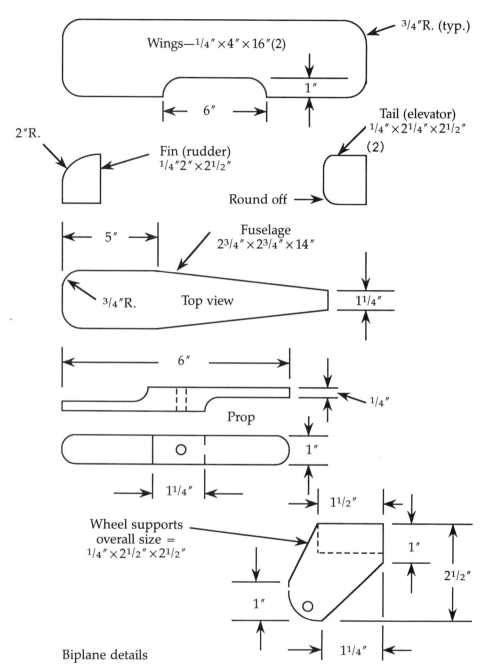

Wings—$1/4'' \times 4'' \times 16''$ (2)

$3/4''$R. (typ.)

$1''$

$6''$

$2''$R.

Fin (rudder)
$1/4'' 2'' \times 2^{1}/_{2}''$

Tail (elevator)
$1/4'' \times 2^{1}/_{4}'' \times 2^{1}/_{2}''$
(2)

Round off →

$5''$

Fuselage
$2^{3}/_{4}'' \times 2^{3}/_{4}'' \times 14''$

$3/4''$R. Top view

$1^{1}/_{4}''$

$6''$

$1/4''$

Prop

$1''$

$1^{1}/_{4}''$

$1^{1}/_{2}''$

Wheel supports
overall size =
$1/4'' \times 2^{1}/_{2}'' \times 2^{1}/_{2}''$

$1''$

$2^{1}/_{2}''$

$1''$

$1^{1}/_{4}''$

Biplane details

Fig. 2-10. Details of the biplane's components.

Form both wings at the same time by holding together two pieces of $1/4$-inch stock. Drill the holes for the struts before separating the pieces. Although the struts are $1/4$-inch dowels, drill the holes for them slightly undersize so they will be a tight fit when assembled with the wings. Regard wings and struts as a sub-assembly that you attach to the fuselage with glue and $3/4$-inch brads.

Make the two legs for the wheel support by holding together two pieces of $1/4$-inch stock. Drill a $5/16$ inch for the axle so it can turn freely. Attach the legs to the crosspiece with glue and 1-inch brads and add the assembly to the fuselage. Use 6d box nails.

The tail structure consists of the three parts that are shown in FIG. 2-10. Put one part of the elevator in place, and add the rudder, and the second elevator piece. All wheels are $1^1/4$ inches in diameter and are mounted on $1/4$-inch dowels. The wheels fit tight on the freely turning axles.

The propeller is made from a piece of $3/4$-inch-×-$3/4$-inch-×-6-inch hardwood. The thickness of each end can be reduced with saw cuts; do final shaping and smooth with sandpaper. Mount the propeller with a #8, 2-inch round-head screw. Drill the hole through the propeller so it can turn freely on the screw, and place a washer between propeller and fuselage.

The biplane in the book was painted one color and decorated with the type of airplane decals that are available in hobby shops.

Pull Wagon

The pull wagon (FIG. 2-11) is not large enough to carry a family of kids, but can tote equipment for a youngster or even such things as garden tools for the grownups. A unique feature is the simplicity of the steering device; it is a plate-

Fig. 2-11. The steering mechanism of the pull wagon is a swivel-type plate caster.

type swivel caster that allows turning the wagon in any direction. Except for the bottom, which is large enough to suggest using plywood, all components can be made of a softwood or hardwood lumber.

Start construction (FIG. 2-12) by cutting a piece of 3/4-inch exterior grade plywood to 11 inches × 16 inches. Use the pad method to shape the two sides, and attach them to the bottom with glue and 5d box nails. Cut the front and back pieces (part #3) and put them in place, again using glue and 5d box nails. Cut the yoke (#4) to size and form the U-shaped opening that will receive the handle. Drill the holes for the dowel on which the handle will pivot and put the yoke in place with glue and four #10, 11/4-inch flat-head wood screws. Make the axle blocks (#5) and drill holes through them so the 1/2-inch dowel that will serve as an axle will turn freely. Drill four pilot holes through each block, locating them so they do not pass through the axle hole, and attach the blocks with glue and 6d

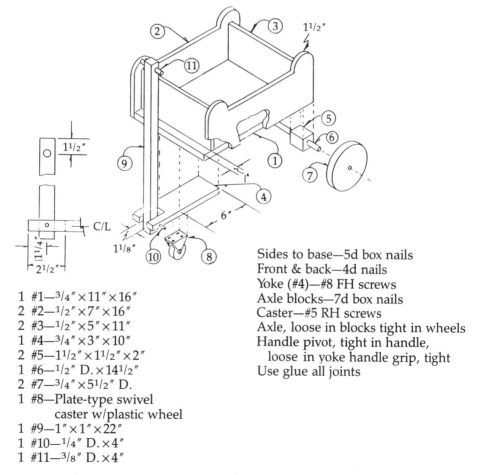

1 #1—3/4″×11″×16″
2 #2—1/2″×7″×16″
2 #3—1/2″×5″×11″
1 #4—3/4″×3″×10″
2 #5—11/2″×11/2″×2″
1 #6—1/2″ D.×141/2″
2 #7—3/4″×51/2″ D.
1 #8—Plate-type swivel
    caster w/plastic wheel
1 #9—1″×1″×22″
1 #10—1/4″ D.×4″
1 #11—3/8″ D.×4″

Sides to base—5d box nails
Front & back—4d nails
Yoke (#4)—#8 FH screws
Axle blocks—7d box nails
Caster—#5 RH screws
Axle, loose in blocks tight in wheels
Handle pivot, tight in handle,
    loose in yoke handle grip, tight
Use glue all joints

Fig. 2-12. The parts that are required, and the assembly of the pull wagon. Casters are available in various sizes and with plastic or rubber wheels.

box nails. Use hardwood for the wheels, forming them with a fly cutter or by hand with a coping saw. The center hole in the wheels should be sized so the wheels will fit tightly on the axle.

Make the handle and drill holes through it for the top grip (#11) and for the bottom pivot pin. The bottom hole should be just large enough so the handle can pivot.

The last step is to attach the caster with four 1-inch round-head screws.

Finish the project with an exterior-type sealer. Apply a coat and sand it smooth when it is dry. Follow with a second coat and a final sanding. There is, of course, no reason why the wagon cannot be painted. If you take that route, start off with a coat of sealer. Remember that paints are also interior and exterior. So choose a type that will hold up in the weather.

Paddle Wheeler

The paddle wheeler, the type that uses a rubberband as a motor (FIG. 2-13), is a classic toy—one that can be enjoyed in a pool or a tub or wherever there is a few inches of water. In "my day," we had them in pairs so we could have races. Testing them today with grandchildren proves that they have not lost their appeal. Construction (FIG. 2-14) is simple, so making a few of them does not add much to production time.

The hull is made of two pieces of $3/4$-inch stock. The bottom part has a 3-inch-$\times$-3-inch notch at the rear to provide room for the paddle wheel. The top part has the same outside shape but its interior is cut away so it forms just a prow and

Fig. 2-13. The paddle wheel boat is an all-time favorite. It can move in just a few inches of water.

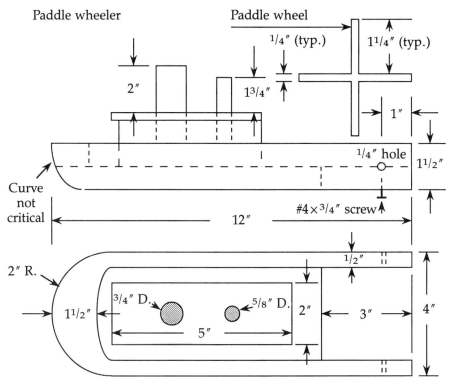

Paddle wheeler

Paddle wheel

1/4″ (typ.)

1 1/4″ (typ.)

2″

1 3/4″

1″

1/4″ hole

1 1/2″

Curve
not
critical

#4 × 3/4″ screw

12″

2″ R.

1/2″

1 1/2″

3/4″ D.

5/8″ D.

2″

3″

4″

5″

Fig. 2-14. How the paddle wheeler is made.

rails. Put the pieces together with waterproof glue and form the curve at the front
end with a rasp and sandpaper or on a belt sander.

The deckhouse is a block that measures 1 1/2 inches × 2 inches × 5 inches.
Top it with a piece of 1/4-inch material that is a bit wider and longer. You can bore

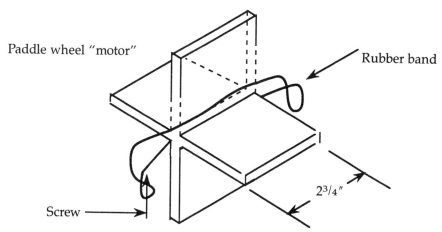

Paddle wheel "motor"

Rubber band

2 3/4″

Screw

Fig. 2-15. Power for the boat is supplied by a heavy rubberband.

the holes for the stacks before or after the deckhouse is attached to the hull with waterproof glue. Make the paddle wheel from a piece of $2^3/4$-inch-$\times$-3-inch-$\times$-3-inch hardwood. Grip the wood in a vise and make saw cuts at right angles to each other to form each of the blades. Use a heavy rubberband for power and install it with the wheel as shown in FIG. 2-15. The boat will move forward or backward depending on how the wheel is wound.

Finish all parts with several coats of exterior-type sealer and with a light sanding between coats and after the final coat.

Yellow Oldster

You cannot make an assortment of playthings for youngsters without including a car. This one (FIG. 2-16) dates back to another time when vehicles were basic and aerodynamics had to do with airplanes. Construction details are offered in FIG. 2-17.

Fig. 2-16. *The yellow oldster is a throwback to the early days of automobiles. No aerodynamics here.*

Start the project with the base, a $3/4$-inch-$\times$-4-inch-$\times$-13-inch piece of softwood that is drilled at each end for the axles. The motor/hood is a solid block that is chamfered along the top edges and installed with glue and 5d box nails driven up through the base. The cab is an assembly of four pieces. The back is solid; front and sides have window openings. The openings will be easy to form

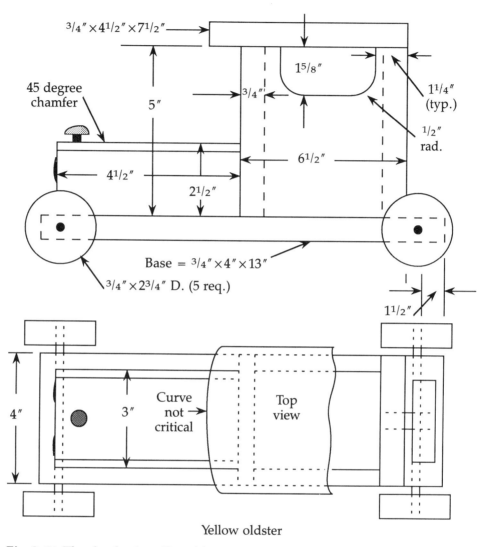

$3/4'' \times 4^{1}/_{2}'' \times 7^{1}/_{2}''$

$1^{5}/_{8}''$

45 degree chamfer

$3/4''$

$5''$

$1^{1}/_{4}''$ (typ.)

$1/2''$ rad.

$4^{1}/_{2}''$

$6^{1}/_{2}''$

$2^{1}/_{2}''$

Base $= 3/4'' \times 4'' \times 13''$

$3/4'' \times 2^{3}/_{4}''$ D. (5 req.)

$1^{1}/_{2}''$

$4''$

$3''$

Curve not → critical

Top view

Yellow oldster

Fig. 2-17. *The plan for the yellow oldster. Headlights and hood ornament are made from wood buttons.*

if you first bore holes to form the round corners and make straight cuts to remove the waste (FIG. 2-18). Attach the cab with glue and nails that are driven up through the base and add the top—this time using 5d finishing nails that are set and concealed with wood dough.

Figure 2-19 details the installation of the wheels. Cutting the axles short allows the use of buttons as hub caps. Buttons are also used as headlights and as the hood ornament. The fifth wheel, the spare tire, is mounted at the back on a short dowel that is set into the rear of the cab.

For panel openings—
drill 1″ holes then saw
on dotted lines

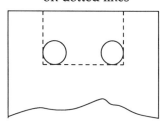

Fig. 2-18. Bored holes will supply smooth, round corners.

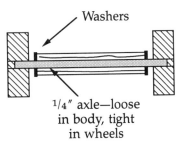

Washers

¼″ axle—loose
in body, tight
in wheels

Button as
hub cap

Fig. 2-19. Wheel assembly for the yellow oldster.

Finish the project with an application of sealer and several coats of paint. The wheel rims—tires—should be painted black.

Pickup Truck

Pickup trucks are perennial favorites. This one (FIG. 2-20) has some detail that adds to its more prosaic chore of toting small objects. Study the details in FIG. 2-21 before beginning construction.

Fig. 2-20. Pickup truck.

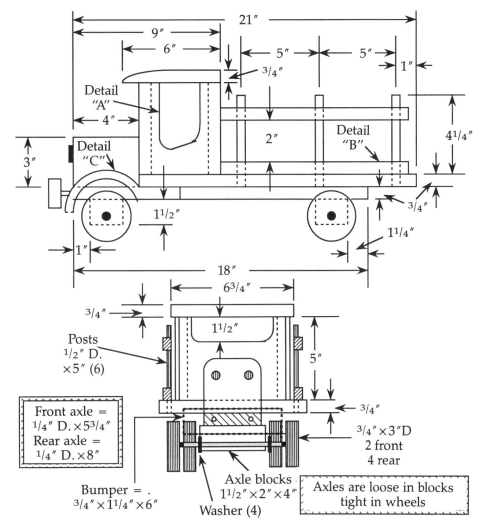

Fig. 2-21. *Assembly details of the pickup truck. The rail and post assemblies can be removable if you don't glue the posts in place.*

The base consists of two pieces; one piece is ³/₄ inch × 8¹/₂ inches × 17 inches, the other measures ³/₄ inch × 3¹/₂ inches × 18 inches. These are centered and joined so the narrow piece extends 4 inches. The motor/hood is a 3-inch-×-3-inch-×-4-inch solid block with rounded top edges. Put it in place with glue and a few 6d box nails that are driven up through the base. The cab that consists of front, back, two sides and a top, is put together as a subassembly as shown in FIG. 2-22A. Use glue and 3d finishing nails when assembling the vertical pieces; use 6d finishing nails when adding the top. Hold the cab tightly against the back of the motor as you secure it with 6d box nails that are driven up through the base.

Make and install the two axle blocks. The holes through the blocks should be $5/16$ inch so the $1/4$-inch dowels that are used as axles will turn freely. Drill pilot holes for the 7d box nails that are used to secure the blocks but locate them carefully so they do not pass through the axle holes.

Drill for, and install, with glue, the six $1/2$-inch dowel posts. The rails, which span the posts, will be easier to make if you follow the ideas that are shown in FIG. 2-22B. Cutting the parts on the centerline after the holes are drilled will produce two parts with semicircular cuts that fit the posts snugly. Attach the rails with a drop of glue and a single $1/2$-inch brad at each contact point.

The fenders are made by following the idea that is shown in FIG. 2-22C. First, use a fly cutter, or work on a scroll saw, to form the 4-inch hole, then shape the outside contour. Sawing on the centerline will produce two identical pieces. Put the fenders in place with glue and 4d finishing nails.

The bumper is rounded off at each end and installed on two $1/4$-inch dowels so that it extends a bit forward from the fenders. The dowels on which the bumper is mounted are glued into holes that are drilled in the front end of the base.

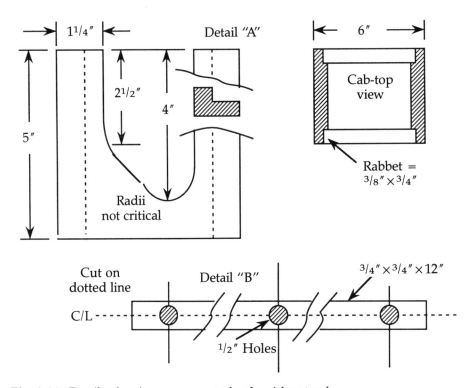

Fig. 2-22. Details of various components for the pickup truck.

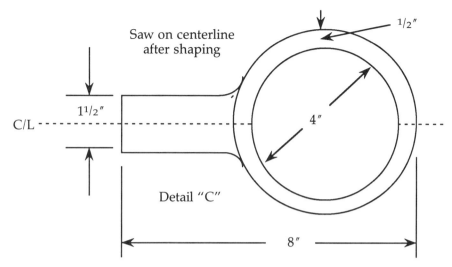

Saw on centerline after shaping

1/2″

1¹/₂″

C/L

4″

Detail "C"

8″

Fig. 2-22. Continued.

Make the six, 3-inch-diameter wheels, two for the front and four for the rear. The wheels are drilled so they will fit tightly on the axles. A drop of glue in the wheel hole as you press them in place is an extra precaution. The project can be painted but settling for a clear finish or just a coat or two of sealer seems appropriate for this type of project.

Pencil Holder

This project (FIG. 2-23) is not a toy, but it will have considerable appeal because of its whimsical ambience.

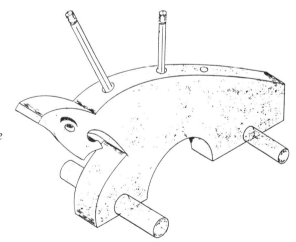

Fig. 2-23. Pencil holder is a nice project for a scroll saw.

Choose a nice piece of hardwood and mark it with the layout that is shown in FIG. 2-24. Drill the pencil holes and the holes for the feet before cutting the profile. Sawing is a natural job for a scroll saw, but it is feasible to work with a saber saw or coping saw.

Sand the sawed edges so they are perfectly smooth and glue the dowel feet in place. Use a clear finish; add eye and brow details with a felt pen. A nice touch would be to add the name of the child by printing or with self-adhesive letters that you can buy in a stationery store.

$3/4''$ stock
$3/8''$ holes for pencils
"Legs" are $1/2''$ D.$\times 4''$ dowels

$1/2''$ squares

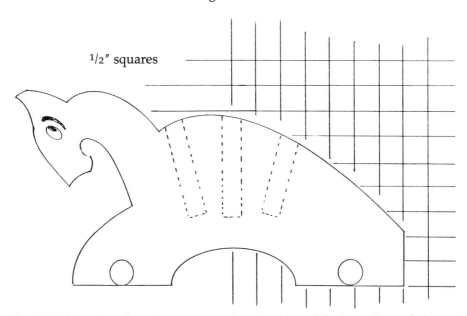

Fig. 2-24. Use the enlarge-by-squares system to make a full-size pattern of the pencil holder. Drill the holes before sawing the profile.

Kitchen Works

Wood is a prime material for kitchen projects. There is certainly plenty of evidence that folks in the past used wood almost exclusively for eating and food preparation, and today, there are many commercial establishments that offer kitchen products in a variety of wood species. Avoid resinous woods and those with an odor (like cedar) when selecting for projects that will come in contact with food. Also, avoid open-grain wood like oak when a project will be left natural since open pores can become contaminated with food particles. Close-grain species like maple, birch, and pine can be used in a natural state without problems.

Softwood, like pine, is suitable for items like ladles or stirrers, but for cutting boards and such, opt for tougher species like birch and maple. Finishing on items that are designed to hold or carry dry foods is optional; stains, lacquers, routine clear, or toned finishes are permissible. A clean, penetrating, clear finish is recommended for items like cutting or chopping boards. Vegetable oil is a common choice, but it can become rancid. A better choice is the mineral oil that is available in pharmacies. Apply it generously and after it has set, wipe off the excess with a lintfree cloth. Repeat the application periodically.

Cutting Boards

Cutting boards can be made of single pieces of solid lumber that are shaped in some geometric fashion like a square or rectangle or circle, or they can have a more interesting motif like the fish design that is offered in FIG. 3-1. Although the plan in FIG. 3-2 calls for 1-inch squares, the project can be larger or smaller. Actually, in a small size, it can serve as part of a wall decor. Construction is straight-

Fig. 3-1. Cutting boards can be made in shapes to suit the imagination.

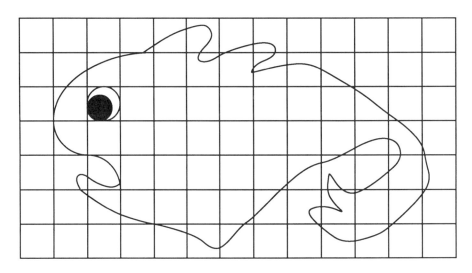

1″ squares

Fig. 3-2. Cutting board with a fish motif. Change the size of the squares if you would like the project to be larger or smaller.

forward, involving sawing the profile with a coping saw or on a scroll saw and sanding edges and surfaces to satin smoothness. If you decide to make a few for decorating, pad pieces of 1/4-inch or 1/2-inch stock so you can produce several with a single sawing operation.

There can be a problem with cutting boards and similar projects that are made of single pieces of lumber. Although the material might be nice and flat to begin with, use and time can cause it to warp. The technique that is shown in FIG. 3-3 is a wise one to use. The parent stock is ripped into several pieces and reassembled with every other strip inverted. This alternates the direction of the annual rings and opposes the inherent tendency of a wide board to warp.

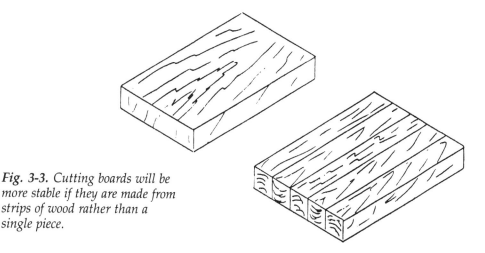

Fig. 3-3. Cutting boards will be more stable if they are made from strips of wood rather than a single piece.

A good bonding with a moisture-resistant or waterproof glue is usually enough to keep the assembly together for a long time, but additional precautions will ensure stability for an heirloom project. Conventional edge-to-edge dowel joints, or end boards are often used. Other methods involve using through dowels and even threaded rods. The threaded-rod idea is certainly the most positive since separation due to glue failure is not likely to occur. The reinforcement ideas are shown in FIG. 3-4.

If you have ever seen a butcher's chopping block, you might have noticed that the wood surface is all endgrain. The toughness of endgrain and the relative ease with which it can be scraped clean are reasons for the idea—an idea that you can apply to a project for home use. The construction, as shown in FIG. 3-5, requires care and effort but the results are worth it. The starting block can be pieces of 2-inch stock, or strips that you cut from a board. When the assembly is ready, it is crosscut into strips of equal width and reassembled after the strips have been flipped 90°. The surface is all endgrain, with the annual rings in each square opposing those in their neighbors.

A butcher-block cutting board is shown in FIG. 3-6 and detailed in FIG. 3-7. An added touch is the contrasting strips that are set into each edge of the project. Form the grooves for the strips after the block is assembled. Use strips that are a bit thicker than the depth of the groove, and sand them flush after the glue dries. The feet are optional. If you add them, do so with glue and a single #10, 1^{1}/$_{2}$-inch

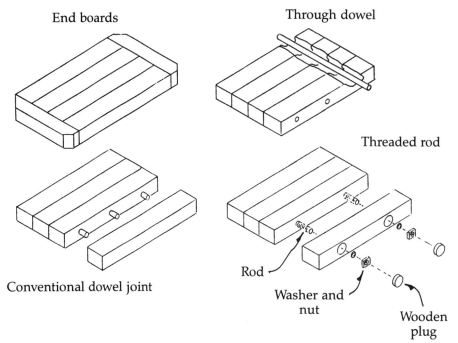

Fig. 3-4. Some of the reinforcement methods used to ensure that cutting boards stay together.

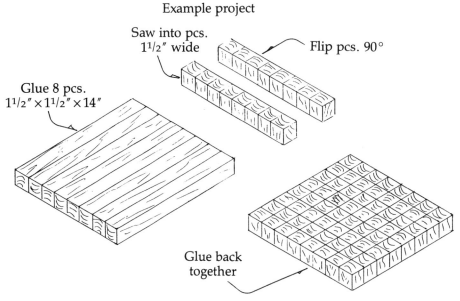

Fig. 3-5. The cutting procedure that is followed when constructing a butcher-block chopping or cutting board.

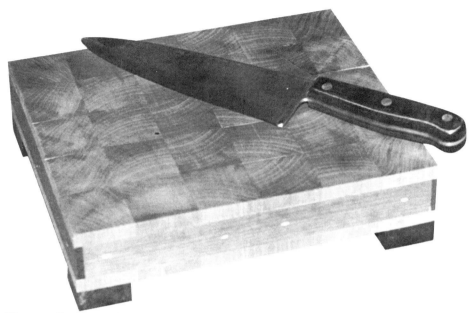

Fig. 3-6. Project made in the butcher-block manner.

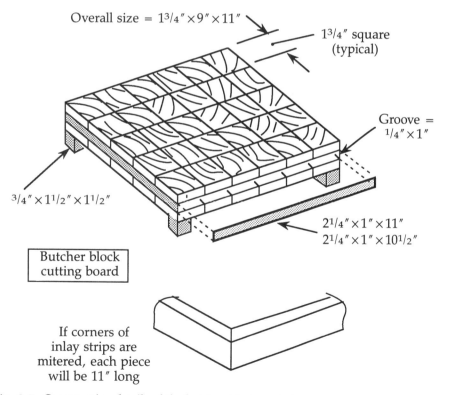

Overall size = $1^3/4'' \times 9'' \times 11''$

$1^3/4''$ square (typical)

Groove = $1/4'' \times 1''$

$3/4'' \times 1^1/2'' \times 1^1/2''$

$2^1/4'' \times 1'' \times 11''$
$2^1/4'' \times 1'' \times 10^1/2''$

Butcher block cutting board

If corners of inlay strips are mitered, each piece will be 11" long

Fig. 3-7. Construction details of the butcher-block project.

flat-head wood screw that is set below the surface of the wood so it cannot scrape any surface the project is placed on.

Cutting boards, when made using the strip technique, do not have to be of one material (FIG. 3-8). Using contrasting materials will make the project unusual. In this case, the species are teak and maple. Once the strips are assembled and the block is cut square, you can form grooves at each end and insert an endboard as shown in FIG. 3-9.

Fig. 3-8. *Cutting boards are more interesting when the slab is made by laminating contrasting wood.*

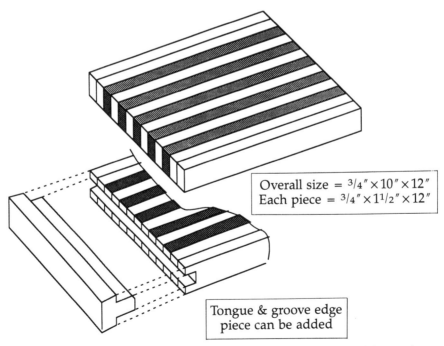

Overall size = $3/4'' \times 10'' \times 12''$
Each piece = $3/4'' \times 1^1/2'' \times 12''$

Tongue & groove edge
piece can be added

Fig. 3-9. *Details for a laminated cutting board. End boards add to stability and appearance.*

Figure 3-10 shows some ways to provide handles for cutting boards. In some cases the design must be provided for during the initial cutting steps, whereas other times, the shaping is done after the project is assembled. Figure 3-11 suggests some ideas for adding feet. Figure 3-12 shows that there can be variations in the shapes of cutting boards.

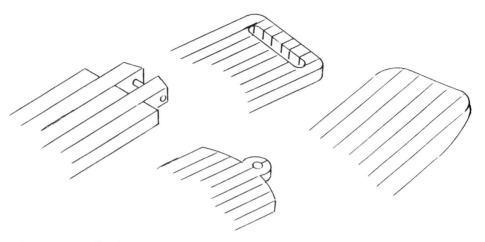

Fig. 3-10. Handles for cutting boards. Tapering ends also provides a means of lifting the board.

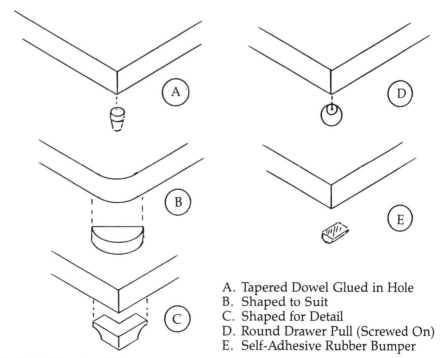

A. Tapered Dowel Glued in Hole
B. Shaped to Suit
C. Shaped for Detail
D. Round Drawer Pull (Screwed On)
E. Self-Adhesive Rubber Bumper

Fig. 3-11. There are different ways to provide a board with feet.

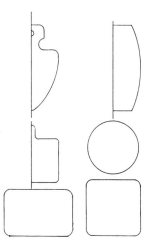

Fig. 3-12. There are many ways to shape a cutting board.

A cutting board becomes a carving board when perimeter shoulders are added to catch juices that flow when slicing poultry or roasts. Figure 3-13 shows one way to accomplish this. The board is trimmed with 3/8-inch or 1/2-inch-thick wood strips that are wider than the thickness of the board by about 1/2 inch. Form a notch in the front strip to serve as a spout, and work with a rasp and sandpaper to round off and smooth all top edges.

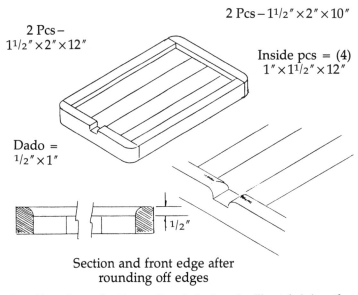

2 Pcs − 1¹/2″ × 2″ × 10″

2 Pcs − 1¹/2″ × 2″ × 12″

Inside pcs = (4)
1″ × 1¹/2″ × 12″

Dado = 1/2″ × 1″

1/2″

Section and front edge after
rounding off edges

Fig. 3-13. Provide a rim and a ''spout'' and the board will catch juices that flow when food is carved.

Paper Napkin Holders

The project shown in FIG. 3-14 is a real quickie and a likely candidate for production output. The shaped piece that is on the squared drawing can be made for both front and back or just for the front if you opt for a plain back. Since the material thickness is only 1/4 inch, you can make a few in a single operation by using the pad-sawing method. Put the parts together using glue and 3/4-inch brads. Set the brads below the surface of the wood and fill the holes with wood dough.

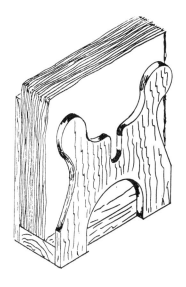

Fig. 3-14. Napkin holder is an easy scroll saw project. Front part can be made in quantity, quickly, by padsawing.

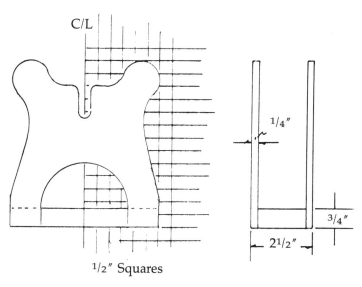

C/L

1/4"

3/4"

2 1/2"

1/2" Squares

You can regard the napkin holder that is shown in FIG. 3-15 as something of an experiment in woodworking since it is carved from a single block of wood. You can use a hardwood or softwood, the difference being that a wood like pine will be easier to work.

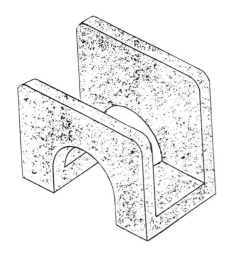

Fig. 3-15. This napkin holder is "carved" from a solid block of wood.

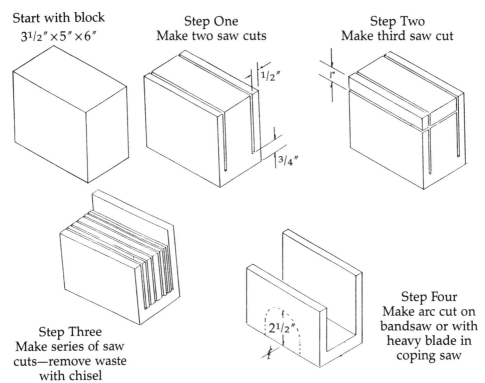

Start with block
3¹/₂″×5″×6″

Step One
Make two saw cuts

¹/₂″

³/₄″

Step Two
Make third saw cut

1″

Step Three
Make series of saw cuts—remove waste with chisel

2¹/₂″

Step Four
Make arc cut on bandsaw or with heavy blade in coping saw

Fig. 3-16. Step-by-step procedure through construction of the one-piece napkin holder.

The steps to follow are detailed in FIG. 3-16. The starting cuts can be made with a handsaw or on a bandsaw. A table saw or radial-arm saw is not recommended since the block of wood is too small for safe handling. If you work on a bandsaw (it should have a 6-inch depth of cut, which is not unusual on a home machine), the waste material (step three) can be removed quickly. The remaining steps after the semicircular cutout is to smooth all edges and to round off the top four corners.

The holder that is shown in FIG. 3-17 can be used indoors but it is more appropriate for a barbecue area where breezes might waft napkins about. Start the project by checking the drawing (FIG. 3-18).

Fig. 3-17. *Napkin holder provides for pepper mill and salt shaker. The design makes the project suitable for use outdoors.*

Size one piece of 3/4 foot pine to 6 1/2 inches × 16 inches and two pieces to 3 3/4 inches × 6 1/2 inches. Form a 2 1/2-inch-diameter hole through the smaller pieces and attach them at the ends of the large piece with glue and 4d finishing nails up through the bottom. Next, cut off the corners of the assembly and round off the forward ends.

Draw the profile of the upright by using the squares method or draw your own curves by using a French-curve drawing tool. The parts can be produced simultaneously if you use the pad-sawing method. Add the two pieces to the base with glue and 6d finishing nails, driving the nails up through the base. The final step is to cut a piece of 1-inch hardwood dowel to a 10-inch length and to round off its ends. Finish the project with several applications of exterior sealer.

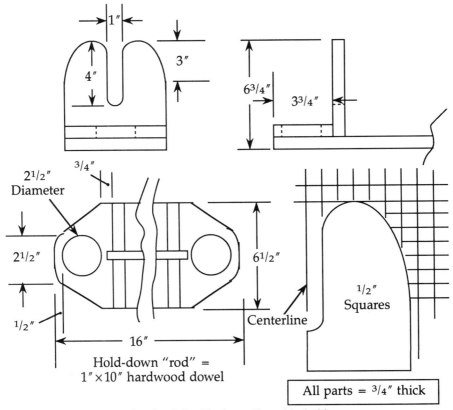

Fig. 3-18. Construction details of the "barbecue" napkin holder.

Napkin Rings

Napkin rings add a nice touch to table settings and provide a means for leaning name tags for table seating. Those shown in FIG. 3-19 are made of aluminum tubing and hardwood. Start work by providing several pieces of ³/₄-inch-×-2-inch-

Fig. 3-19. Napkin rings made of hardwood and aluminum tubing.

×-4-inch hardwood and boring a 1¹/₂-inch hole through each of them (FIG. 3-20).

Separate the parts by sawing on the centerline of the hole and sand the parts to the contours that are shown in the drawing. Aluminum tubing can easily be sawed with a regular wood-cutting blade on a bandsaw or with a coping saw or backsaw. Slice the rings so they are about ¹/₁₆ inch wider than needed so they can be sanded flush after they are installed. Attach them to the wood with an epoxy adhesive. After sanding, use a sharp knife or chisel on the edges of the aluminum rings to remove the slight burrs that sanding will leave.

The rings that are shown in FIG. 3-21 are all wood and can be made in mass production by following the procedure that is suggested in FIG. 3-22. Drilling the holes in the starting block is best done on a drill press. If you work with hand tools, drill pilot holes through each edge of the block and enlarge them. Holes of

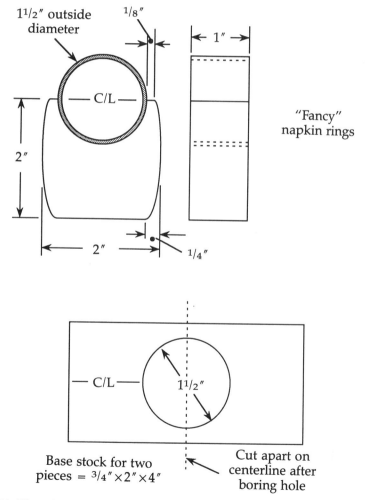

Fig. 3-20. How the aluminum and hardwood napkin rings are made.

this size are not too difficult to form with a brace and bit. After drilling, the block is sawed apart as shown in the drawing and each piece is sanded so the top edge is round or shaped something like a Gothic arch.

Both styles can be finished with varnish. The aluminum rings will take on a satiny texture if you scrub them with fine steel wool. This should be done before applying the final finish.

Fig. 3-21. All-wood napkin rings.

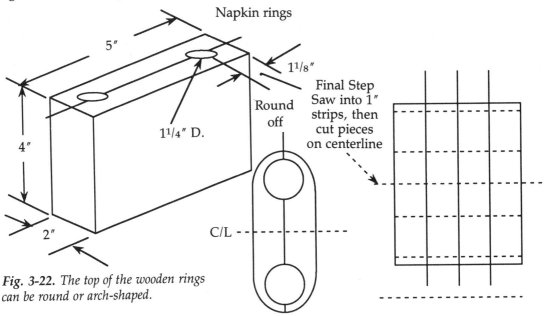

Napkin rings

5″

1¹/₈″

1¹/₄″ D.

4″

2″

Round off

Final Step
Saw into 1″ strips, then cut pieces on centerline

C/L

Fig. 3-22. The top of the wooden rings can be round or arch-shaped.

Coffee Mug Tree

Coffee drinkers enjoy having special mugs, often personalized. A coffee tree, like the one in FIG. 3-23, is a nice way to store or display them. Start the project by providing the post and cutting four 3⅝-inch lengths of ½-inch dowel. The angular holes for the pegs can be drilled accurately if you make the guide that is shown in FIG. 3-24. Chamfer both ends of the pegs and put them in place with a drop of glue.

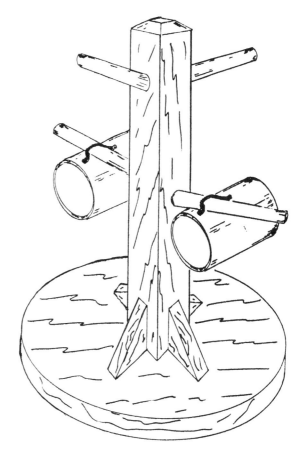

Fig. 3-23. Coffee cup tree.

Form the circular base and attach the post with glue and a single #8×2-inch flat-head wood screw that is driven up through the bottom. The triangular pieces are optional but they do add some visual stability. If you decide to add them, just use glue in the connection. You can do some extra things to the project. For example, shape the perimeter of the base with a router, or simply round it off by using a rasp and sandpaper.

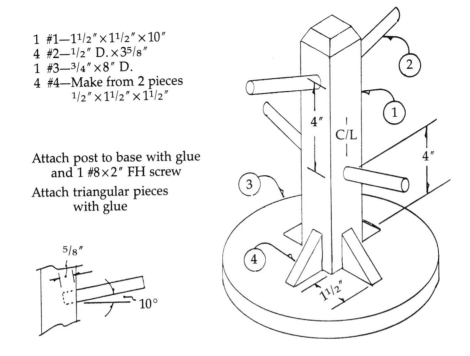

1 #1—$1^1/_2'' \times 1^1/_2'' \times 10''$
4 #2—$^1/_2''$ D. $\times 3^5/_8''$
1 #3—$^3/_4'' \times 8''$ D.
4 #4—Make from 2 pieces
      $^1/_2'' \times 1^1/_2'' \times 1^1/_2''$

Attach post to base with glue
and 1 #8×2" FH screw

Attach triangular pieces
with glue

How to drill angular hole

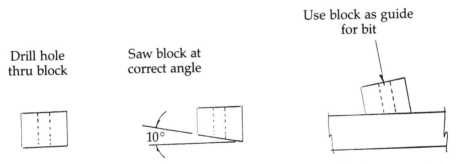

Drill hole
thru block

Saw block at
correct angle

Use block as guide
for bit

Fig. 3-24. *How the coffee cup tree is put together. The angular holes that are required can be drilled accurately if you make the guide block suggested here.*

Wooden Utensils

An interesting name for making household wooden cooking items is *treening*, a term derived from an old English word *treow*, which means wood or tree. Making utensils like ladles, spoons, and forks, goes back in time. Today, such items are used by choice, not necessity. Wood does not conduct much heat and will not add flavor to food. Pine is nice to use since it is easy to work with and durable. Harder woods like maple and birch are probably best for items like spreaders and stirrers.

Forks and ladles like those that are shown in FIGS. 3-25 through 3-27, are among the most popular treening projects. The best basic-shaping method is to do compound sawing, a technique that is usually associated with a bandsaw but which, on projects of this nature, is feasible enough with a coping saw that is equipped with a heavy blade (FIG. 3-28).

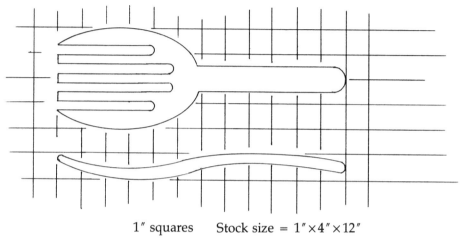

1" squares   Stock size = 1" × 4" × 12"

Fig. 3-25. Wooden fork project.

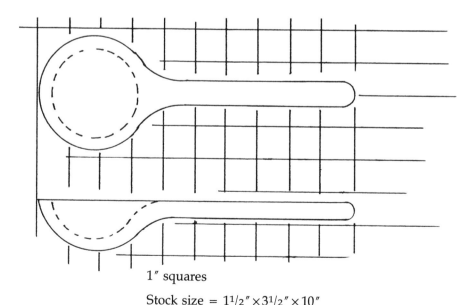

1" squares

Stock size = 1¹/2" × 3¹/2" × 10"

Fig. 3-26. Ladle project with round scoop.

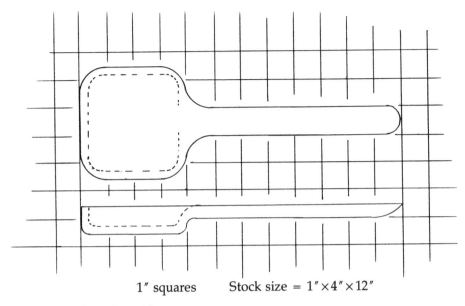

1" squares   Stock size = 1" × 4" × 12"

Fig. 3-27. Ladle project with square scoop.

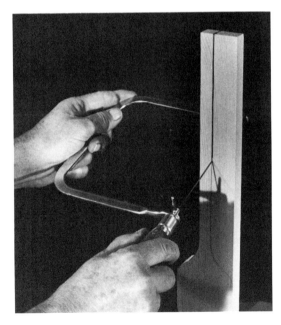

Fig. 3-28. Coping saw with a heavy blade can be used to shape the profiles of the treen projects.

Compound sawing starts by drawing the top and side profiles of the project on the stock (FIG. 3-29). After the top profile is cut, the waste pieces are returned and held in place with tape so the stock will have a flat surface for sawing the side profile. This is important for powersawing. If you are working with a handsaw, just sketch the side profile on the stock after the top profile has been sawed.

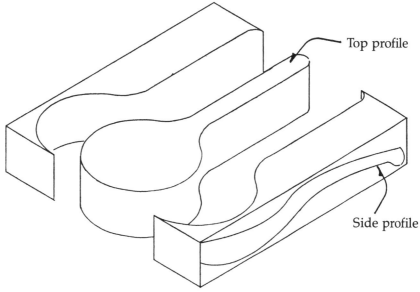

Fig. 3-29. Compound sawing is a bandsaw technique that can be used to cut top and side profiles.

When forming the tines on forks, first drill endholes and make parallel saw cuts as shown in FIG. 3-30. This will leave smooth radii in the openings between the tines. The hollows in projects like ladles can be formed with a curved carving gouge (FIG. 3-31). Incise the perimeter of the hollow with a sharp knife, and gouge out chips that are no more than $1/16$-inch or $1/8$-inch thick. Work from the ends to the center so all cuts will be parallel with the grain. After basic shapes are formed, the final rounding and smoothing of surfaces and edges is accomplished with rasps and files and sandpaper.

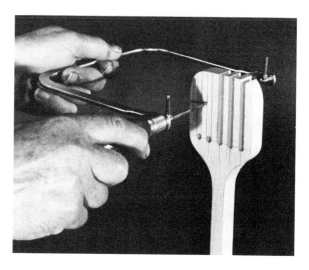

Fig. 3-30. Drilling end holes first will make sawing tines a lot easier.

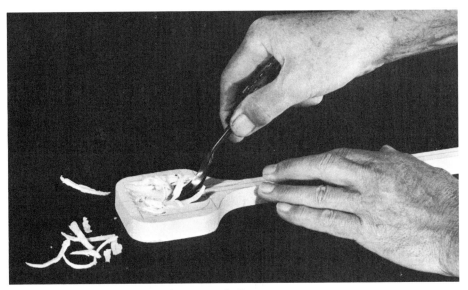

Fig. 3-31. *Use a small, curved gouge to hollow scoop areas.*

Designs for stirrers are offered in FIG. 3-32. These utensils always have openings through the blades so they can pass through soups or sauces more easily. One way to make them in quantity is to saw the profile and to form the opening or tines in wood about $1^{1}/_{2}$ inches thick. Resaw the wood into three separate pieces.

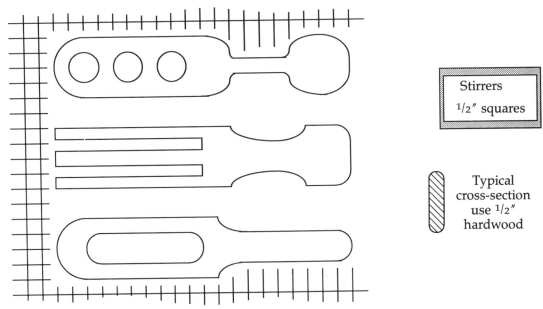

Stirrers

$^{1}/_{2}"$ squares

Typical cross-section use $^{1}/_{2}"$ hardwood

Fig. 3-32. *Designs for stirrers.*

A choice of spreaders is offered in FIG. 3-33. It is probably not a good idea to shape them with sharp edges even though the drawings show them this way. A knife edge, even on hardwood, would be too fragile. It would be better to taper them to about 1/16 inch and round off the edge.

Pay special attention to sanding treen projects. End up with a fine abrasive so all areas will be satiny smooth. Most projects of this nature are left in natural state. Dampening them with a cloth and sanding to remove any fibers that rise is a good idea.

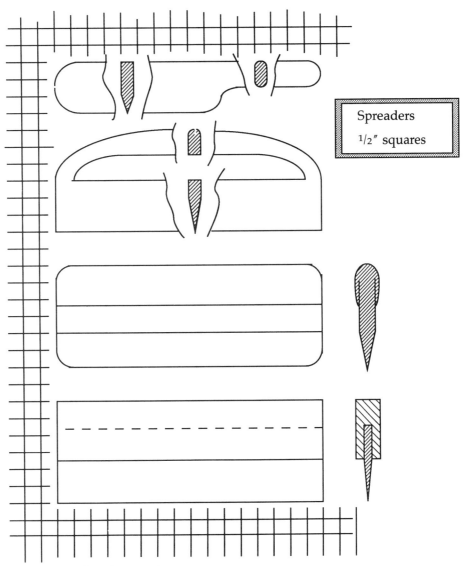

Fig. 3-33. *Designs for spreaders.*

Serving Trays

Wooden serving trays fall into the treen category even though they are not confined to use in the kitchen. A fairly basic design, one that can be from a block of 1½-inch-thick softwood or hardwood is shown in FIG. 3-34. The project can be made larger or its shape can be altered by changing the squares system that is suggested in FIG. 3-35. The interior is cut away by using the piercing system. That

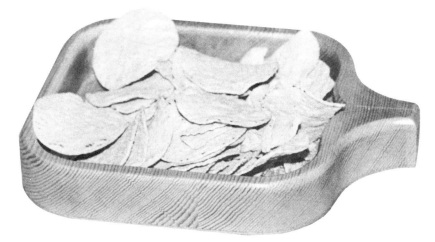

Fig. 3-34. *Simple tray can be cut from a single piece of 1½ inch-thick soft wood or hardwood.*

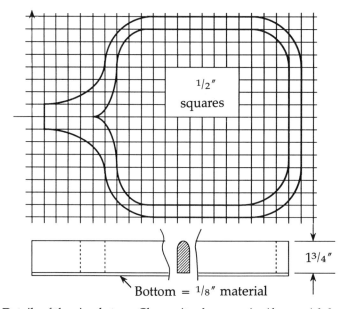

½″

squares

1¾″

Bottom = ⅛″ material

Fig. 3-35. *Details of the simple tray. Change its shape or size if you wish by using different squares when transferring the pattern.*

is, holes are drilled in waste areas so a saw can be passed through before the blade is secured in chucks. The technique applies whether you do sawing with a scroll saw or a coping saw.

The bottom is a piece of 1/8-inch plywood that is just glued in place. Cut the plywood a bit oversize so it can be sanded flush with the frame after the glue dries.

A technique to avoid the piercing chore on this type of project is demonstrated in FIG. 3-36. The entry cut allows making the inside cutout without fuss. The kerf is closed by gluing.

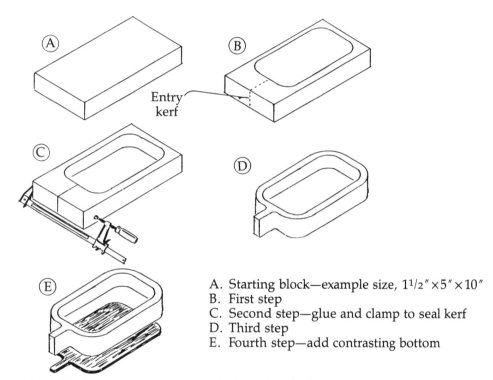

A. Starting block—example size, 1^1/$_2$"×5"×10"
B. First step
C. Second step—glue and clamp to seal kerf
D. Third step
E. Fourth step—add contrasting bottom

Fig. 3-36. A system you can use to eliminate the piercing chore when making trays.

"Stone" Tray

Actually, the tray in FIG. 3-37 is wood but it has a stone appearance and texture because it was finished with a new product called Fleck Stone. The finish, which is available in art supply stores and craft shops, comes in spray cans; one that supplies the finish, the other that supplies a protective coat. It is an easy way to give a project a distinctive appearance.

The plan for the tray is in FIG. 3-38. Do the cutting on stock that is 1^1/$_2$ inches thick and glue on a 1/4-inch or 1/2-inch bottom. Follow the application instructions that are on the Fleck Stone containers.

Fig. 3-37. Tray has a unique appearance because of the special Fleck-Stone finish. The text tells about the new product.

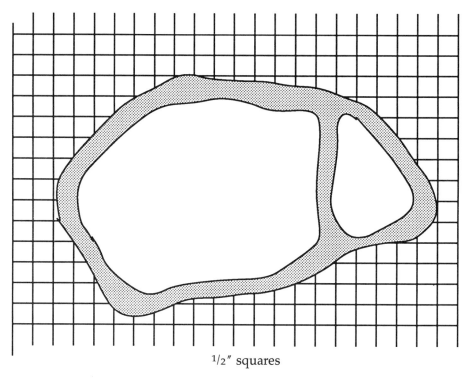

¹/2″ squares

Fig. 3-38. Pattern for the ''stone'' tray.

Tray with Handle

This tray (FIG. 3-39), differs from the usual in that the hollows for holding items are formed by boring blind holes. The holes will be easy to form if you have a Forstner bit that is about 2³/4 inches in diameter. Another system is to make circular cuts with a hole saw or fly cutter and remove the waste with chisels.

The drawing (FIG. 3-40) offers an alternate method but this also requires tools that can form large holes. If drilling the holes is not an option for you, think about forming the holes on a scroll saw or with a coping saw.

The handle is cut from a piece of 1/2-inch stock and is attached with glue. The book project was made with maple and finished with a red mahogany stain, but you may have other ideas.

Fig. 3-39. Tray with handle. Hollows are formed by boring blind holes.

"Woven" Tray

The project shown in FIGS. 3-41 and 3-42 is a little departure from routine tray design. Glue two 3/4-inch- × -6-inch-wide pieces of wood together for the base. If you want to skip the gluing chore, reduce the diameter of the circle to 11¼ inches so a single piece can be used. In this case, reduce the radius of the circle on which the holes are drilled so their edge distance will remain 1 inch.

Use a protractor to mark the hole locations and drill 1/2-inch holes that are 3/8-inch deep. You can use ordinary dowel for the posts but commercial, striated

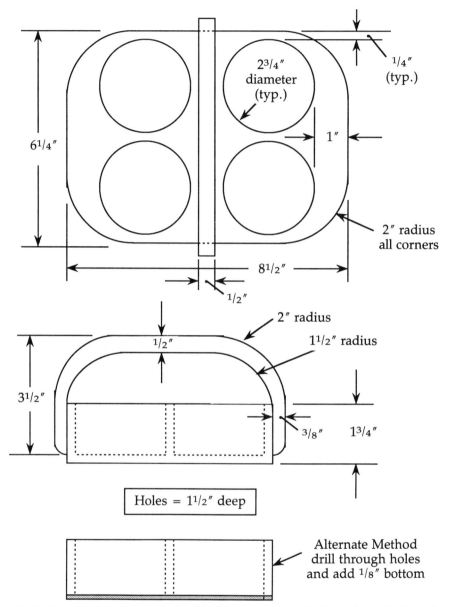

2³/₄″ diameter (typ.)

1″

¼″ (typ.)

6¹/₄″

2″ radius all corners

8¹/₂″

¹/₂″

¹/₂″

2″ radius

1¹/₂″ radius

3¹/₂″

³/₈″   **1³/₄″**

Holes = 1¹/₂″ deep

Alternate Method
drill through holes
and add ¹/₈″ bottom

Fig. 3-40. *Details of the tray with handle. The alternate method can be used if you form the holes with a coping saw or on a scroll saw.*

pegs are appropriate and add a decorative touch. Install the pegs by tapping them into place after coating the insertion end lightly with glue.

Finish the project with a coat or two of varnish before doing the weaving. The kind of cord used for macrame is a good choice but there are many options:

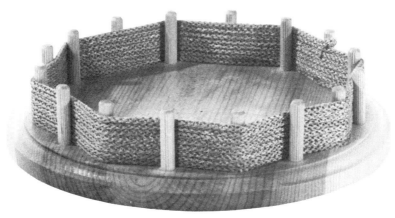

Fig. 3-41. Tray with "woven" sides. Perimeter of the base can be shaped or just rounded off.

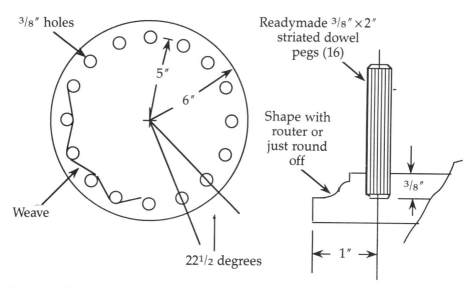

Fig. 3-42. How the woven tray is made. Striated dowel pegs add a decorative detail.

twine, heavy cord, and so on. Use a tack to secure the material where the weaving starts and ends.

A Duo for Crackers

The cracker trough (FIG. 3-43) requires just four pieces of wood. Start with two pieces, 1/2 inch × 2 1/2 inches × 5 inches. Mark the profile on one piece and hold the pieces together with doubleface tape or by tacknailing so you can cut them simultaneously. Use plywood for the sides if you have trouble finding solid wood

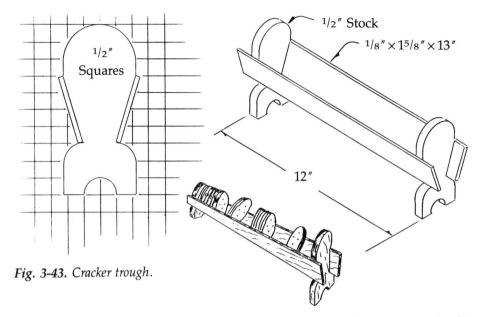

Fig. 3-43. Cracker trough.

that is 1/8 inch thick. Shops that offer materials for model makers supply thin wood.

Install the sides by using glue and 3/4-inch brads. You can add a decorative touch if you substitute brass escutcheon pins for the brads. A coat of varnish or an application or two of sealer will finish the project nicely.

Another way to serve crackers is to tote them about in the wheelbarrow shown in FIG. 3-44. Start the project by making the substructure (FIG. 3-45), put-

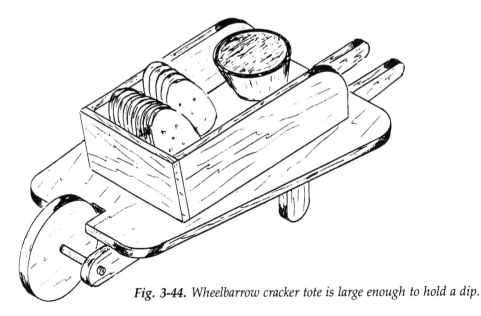

Fig. 3-44. Wheelbarrow cracker tote is large enough to hold a dip.

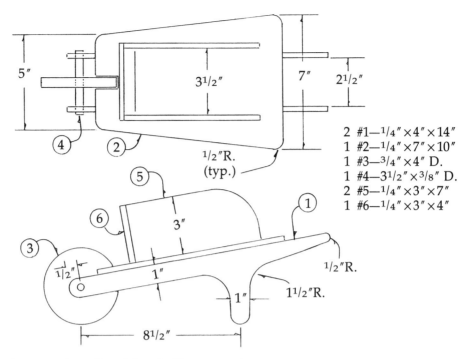

5"

$3^1/2$"

7" $2^1/2$"

④   ②

$^1/2$"R.
(typ.)

⑤

⑥

3"

③

$^1/2$"   1"

⑧$^1/2$"

$^1/2$"R.

1" $1^1/2$"R.

①

2 #1—$^1/4$"×4"×14"
1 #2—$^1/4$"×7"×10"
1 #3—$^3/4$"×4" D.
1 #4—$3^1/2$"×$^3/8$" D.
2 #5—$^1/4$"×3"×7"
1 #6—$^1/4$"×3"×4"

Fig. 3-45. *Assembly of the wheelbarrow cracker tote.*

ting two pieces of wood together as a pad so the two parts can be cut in one operation. Next, make the base (part #2), shaping it as shown in the drawing and
notching it at the front to provide freedom for the wheel. Attach the base to the
legs with glue and $^3/4$-inch brads driven down from the top. Put parts #5 and 6
together as a subassembly and glue and clamp to attach it to the base.

Make the wheel by using a fly cutter or by sawing. Drill the axle hole in the
wheel a bit larger than $^3/8$ inch. The wheel will turn on the axle, which should fit
tightly in the holes in the legs.

Trivets

Trivets, like the one in FIG. 3-46, can be made quickly and easily by making saw
cuts that run at right angles to each other into opposite surfaces of a slab of
wood. The sawing is done best on a table saw or radial-arm saw.

The cuts (kerfs) can be as wide as the saw blade will cut or you can broaden
them by working with a dado assembly. The idea, shown in FIG. 3-47, is to make
the cuts a bit deeper than half the thickness of the stock. Thus, openings appear
wherever the cuts cross.

Another way to make trivets is shown in FIG. 3-48. This system is more complicated and calls for careful layout and sawing since the strips cut from the part
that is made in step one must mesh precisely when they are reassembled. The

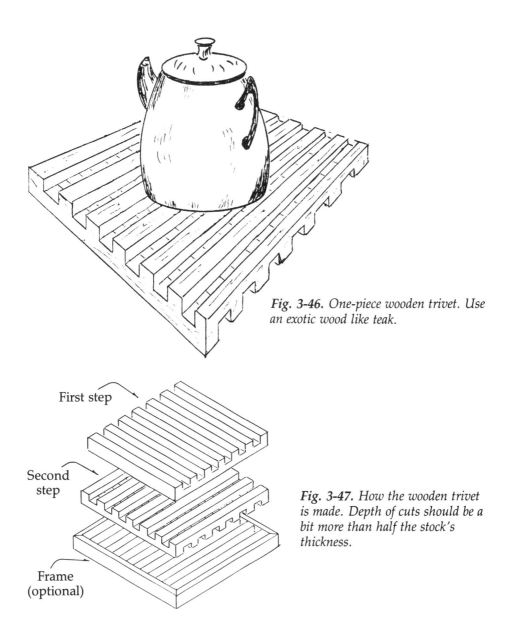

Fig. 3-46. One-piece wooden trivet. Use an exotic wood like teak.

First step

Second step

Frame (optional)

Fig. 3-47. How the wooden trivet is made. Depth of cuts should be a bit more than half the stock's thickness.

technique does offer the opportunity to do something different. Do the kerfing that is called for in step one in pieces of contrasting wood. Alternate the strips when you do the final assembly. Choose an exotic hardwood when making wooden trivets. Teak is a popular choice.

A different approach to making trivets was adopted when the sample that is shown in FIG. 3-49 was designed. You can use the dimensions offered in FIG. 3-50, or decide your own length and width. First, cut the major piece of wood to size

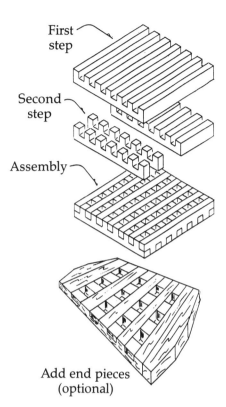

First step

Second step

Assembly

Add end pieces
(optional)

Fig. 3-48. Another way to make wooden trivets. All cutting must be done very carefully.

Fig. 3-49. Aluminum-veneered trivet looks like it was made with metal tiles.

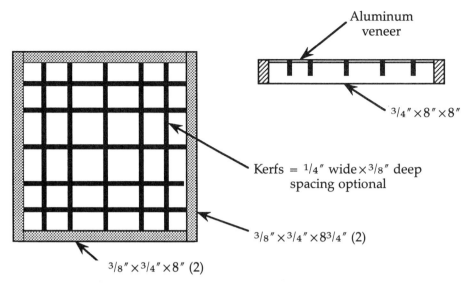

Fig. 3-50. *"Tiles" appear when the aluminum-veneered slab is kerfed. Choose your own pattern for the saw cuts.*

and, using contact cement, veneer it with aluminum. The metal can be the do-it-yourself type, which is available in home-supply centers, or something heavier. Check the yellow pages under *metals* for other sources of supply.

The next step is to cut intersecting kerfs about 1/4 inch deep, spacing them uniformly, or to produce a particular pattern. The aluminum will cut easily and with minimum burring if you use a smooth-cutting, carbide-tipped saw blade. Run over the sawed edges with a strip of sandpaper or even a smooth file so they will not be sharp. The final step is to frame the project with strips of 3/8-inch-thick wood. You can leave the shiny finish of the aluminum or make it more satiny by rubbing with emery paper or fine steel wool.

Towel Rack

Racks for paper towels are popular kitchen accessories but the usual commercial ones are plastic and prosaic. Our project is more interesting and includes a shelf for displaying interesting kitchen bric-a-brac (FIGS. 3-51 and 3-52).

Cut the back piece to overall size and form the top scallops and the bottom cutout. Produce the two pieces that are required for the sides by pad sawing. Drill the hole for the towel bar before you separate the pieces.

Attach the sides to the back with glue and three or four 6d finishing nails. Cut the shelf so it will fit snugly in place and fasten it as you did the sides. The final part is the towel bar, which is just a 14-inch length of 3/4-inch hardwood dowel. The bar should fit the holes snugly enough so it cannot roll out of place when the towels are pulled off.

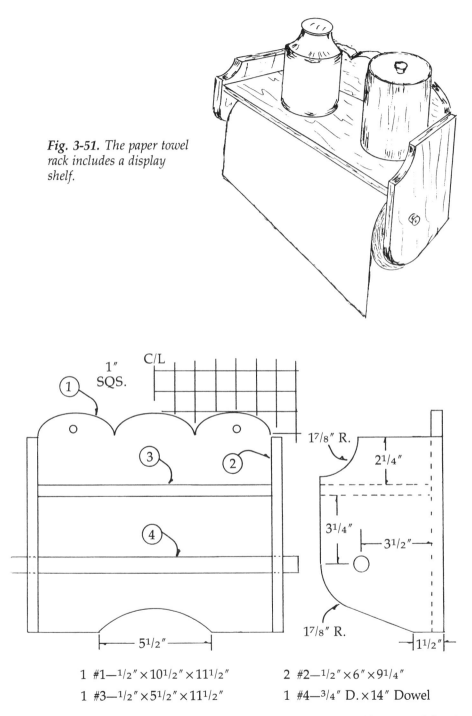

Fig. 3-51. *The paper towel rack includes a display shelf.*

1" SQS.

C/L

① 1

③ 3

② 2

④ 4

$1^7/_8$" R.

$2^1/_4$"

$3^1/_4$"

$3^1/_2$"

$1^7/_8$" R.

$1^1/_2$"

$5^1/_2$"

1 #1—$^1/_2$" × $10^1/_2$" × $11^1/_2$"   2 #2—$^1/_2$" × 6" × $9^1/_4$"

1 #3—$^1/_2$" × $5^1/_2$" × $11^1/_2$"   1 #4—$^3/_4$" D. × 14" Dowel

Fig. 3-52. *How the towel rack goes together. Clear pine is a suitable material for the project.*

Set all nail heads below the surface of the wood and conceal them with wood dough. Paint or stain the project to suit the decor of the kitchen. The project can be mounted on a wall by using the type of hooks that are usually used to hang picture frames. If necessary, bend the hooks a bit so they will slip through the holes in the back of the unit.

4

Three for
the Birds

Most people enjoy playing host to birds and are amply rewarded for their efforts with pleasant sights and sounds. Making a feeder as a gift or for your own yard is a nice workshop activity. Homes for birds must often be designed for specific species; shape, size, entry, roost, can be important, but you can be more flexible with feeders since they are not intended as habitats. Similarities do occur though in terms of building materials and the fasteners to use.

Wood is by far the wisest choice since its naturalness suits outdoor settings, and applicable species are easy to work with. Pine, yellow poplar, and cypress (the most durable) are good choices. Feeders can be painted in muted tones of grays, greens, or browns to blend with surroundings and to bolster weathering qualities, but natural finishes are also desirable. An interesting procedure is to use the project unfinished for a spell to allow it to weather. Then, apply several coats of exterior sealer.

Fasteners can be nails or screws but should be noncorrosive or protectively coated. Galvanized or aluminum nails will do. Box nails are a good choice since exposed nailheads are not objectionable on this type of project. Use waterproof glue in all joints.

Skyscraper

The feeder shown in FIG. 4-1 consists of two assemblies; the roof structure, and the seed container and platform that comprise the bottom component. As shown in FIG. 4-2, the parts are joined by a heavy dowel that passes through holes in the

Fig. 4-1. The skyscraper.

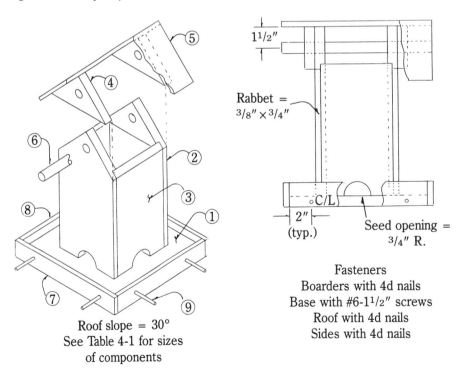

Roof slope = 30°
See Table 4-1 for sizes
of components

$1^{1}/_{2}''$

Rabbet =
$^{3}/_{8}'' \times ^{3}/_{4}''$

C/L

$2''$
(typ.)

Seed opening =
$^{3}/_{4}''$ R.

Fasteners
Boarders with 4d nails
Base with #6-1$^{1}/_{2}''$ screws
Roof with 4d nails
Sides with 4d nails

Fig. 4-2. Assembly details for the skyscraper bird feeder.

assemblies. Removing the dowel releases the lower structure so it can be filled with seed. The sizes of the parts that are required are listed in TABLE 4-1.

Table 4-1. Materials List.

Req'd.	Part No.	Size
1	1	$3/4'' \times 10'' \times 10''$
2	2	$3/4'' \times 5'' \times 12''$
2	3	$3/4'' \times 51/4'' \times 10''$
2	4	$3/4'' \times 3'' \times 6''$
2	5	$3/8'' \times 51/2'' \times 103/4''$
1	6	$3/4''$ D. $\times 10''$
2	7	$3/8'' \times 13/4'' \times 103/4''$
2	8	$3/8'' \times 13/4'' \times 10''$
8	9	$1/4''$ D. $\times 31/2''$

Start by making the parts for the seed box (#2, 3). A way to make these parts so the semicircular seed outlet will be easy to produce is shown in FIG. 4-3. Cut the parts more than twice as long as they are needed and bore a $13/4$-inch hole on the centerline. Halving the stock produces two parts with semicircular openings. Hold the sides (#2) together when drilling the hole for the dowel. Form the rabbets that are required in the sides before cutting the 30° roof slope. Use a rasp and sandpaper to conform the top edge of the ends (#3) to the roof slope after the four pieces have been joined with glue and 4d nails.

Cut the platform (#1) to size and add the border pieces. Drill the holes for the dowel before joining base and seed box with glue and #6 $11/2$-inch flat-head screws.

Cut the end parts of the roof so they conform to the shape of the box sides and drill the holes for the dowel. Use an exterior grade of plywood for the roof

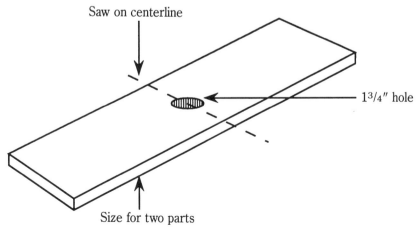

Saw on centerline

$13/4''$ hole

Size for two parts

Fig. 4-3. Easy way to form semicircular openings for the skyscraper project.

pieces (#5) and put them in place with glue and nails. Be generous when applying glue along the ridge line. To guard against leakage you might apply a bead of caulking to the underside of the ridge joint.

Sand the dowel connector (#6), if necessary, so it will slide easily through the holes. Cut parts #9 to length and tap them into place after placing a drop of glue in the holes. Use screw eyes on the project, and light, galvanized chain or wire for hanging.

Ranch House

The ranch house is a heavier project that seems to be appreciated by larger birds, like doves, since they can land on it without it becoming a seesaw. Of course, smaller birds, as you can see in FIG. 4-4, do not object to it either.

Fig. 4-4. The ranch house.

Figure 4-5 shows how the project is assembled, whereas TABLE 4-2 lists the sizes of the components. The feed box has notches at the base of each of its sides, and a sliding top that makes it easy to supply seeds. Part #2 is rabbeted at each end to receive the sides; all three pieces are grooved at the top edge for the sliding cover. Part #4, which completes the box, is cut shorter so the cover can slide over it.

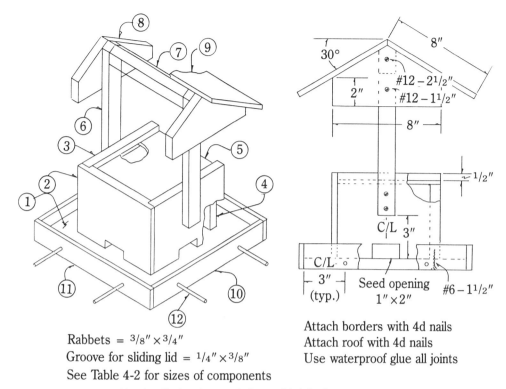

Rabbets = $3/8'' \times 3/4''$
Groove for sliding lid = $1/4'' \times 3/8''$
See Table 4-2 for sizes of components

Attach borders with 4d nails
Attach roof with 4d nails
Use waterproof glue all joints

Fig. 4-5. Assembly details for the ranch house bird feeder.

Table 4-2. Materials List.

Req'd.	Part No.	Size
1	1	$3/4'' \times 12' \times 12''$
1	2	$3/4'' \times 6'' \times 8''$
2	3	$3/4'' \times 6'' \times 75/8''$
1	4	$3/4'' \times 51/4'' \times 61/2''$
1	5	$1/4'' \times 71/4'' \times 75/8''$
2	6	$3/4'' \times 11/4'' \times 12''$
1	7	$11/4'' \times 2'' \times 8''$
2	8	$3/4'' \times 4'' \times 8''$
2	9	$3/8'' \times 8'' \times 14''$
2	10	$3/8'' \times 13/4'' \times 12''$
2	11	$3/8'' \times 13/4'' \times 123/4$
8	12	$1/4''$ D. $\times 41/2''$

The top structure, roof and posts, can be assembled as a unit. Start with the posts and ridge (#6 and 7), putting them together and forming a slope of 30° from centerline to edges. This can be accomplished by sawing if you work carefully, by planing, or with a rasp and sandpaper. Make the peaked sides (#8) and attach them to the posts with glue and the flat-head screws that are listed on the assembly drawing. The unit will be finished when you add the two pieces that form the roof (#9).

Cut the platform (#1) to size and, after adding the border pieces and drilling the holes for the dowels, attach it to the feed box with glue and #6 1¹/₂-inch flat-head screws. Secure the top structure to the feed box with glue and two #6 1¹/₂-inch flat-head screws through each post.

Finish the project by cutting the eight dowels (#12) to length and tapping them into place after putting a drop of glue in the holes. Install screw eyes at the top for hanging the feeder.

Penthouse

The penthouse bird feeder (FIG. 4-6) is suitable for mounting on a tall post. The project can be secured to a wooden or a pipe post by using the ideas that are

Fig. 4-6. Penthouse bird feeder.

shown in FIG. 4-7. Whether you use wood or a pipe, the support will have maximum security if you install it in the ground by following the procedure shown in FIG. 4-8.

The parts are put together as shown in FIG. 4-9; TABLE 4-3 lists the sizes of the components. Hold the two pieces that are required for the sides (#1) together with tape or by tacknailing. Saw the part to shape and drill the hole for the dowel before separating the pieces.

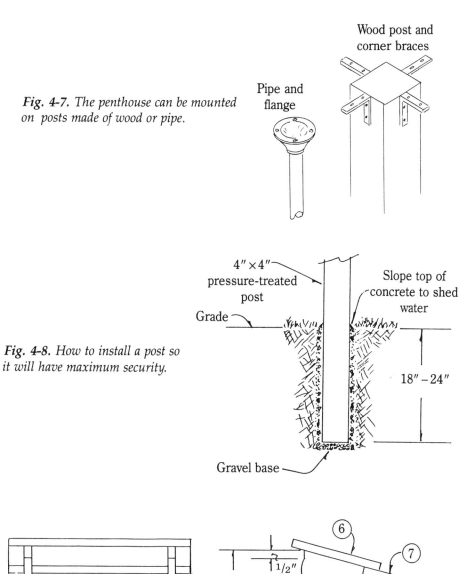

Fig. 4-7. *The penthouse can be mounted on posts made of wood or pipe.*

Pipe and flange

Wood post and corner braces

Fig. 4-8. *How to install a post so it will have maximum security.*

4″ × 4″ pressure-treated post

Grade

Slope top of concrete to shed water

18″ − 24″

Gravel base

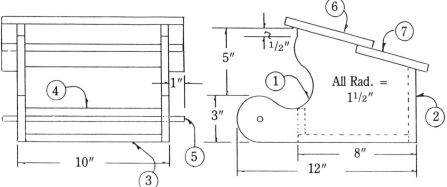

4

10″

5

3

1″

5″

3″

12″

1/2″

1

All Rad. = 1½″

8″

6

7

2

Fig. 4-9. *How the penthouse project is assembled.*

Table 4-3. Materials List.

Req'd	Part No.	Size
2	1	$1/2'' \times 8'' \times 12''$
1	2	$1/2'' \times 5'' \times 9''$
1	3	$1/2'' \times 8'' \times 9''$
1	4	$1/2'' \times 13/4'' \times 9''$
1	5	$3/8''$ D. $\times 12''$
1	6	$1/2'' \times 6'' \times 12''$
1	7	$1/2'' \times 5'' \times 12''$

Use ext. grade plywood, assemble with waterproof glue and use 4d aluminum nails. Roof slope = 15°.

Cut the back, bottom, and front (#2, #3, #4) to size and assemble them together with the sides. Use a plane or a rasp to conform the top edge of the back to the slope of the roof. Add the two roof pieces and the dowel (#5), and the project is complete.

Feeders, or birdhouses, that are mounted on posts should be provided with some security so predators cannot climb up. A solution is to make a sheet metal inverted cone that is nailed or screwed at about the midpoint of the post.

5

Shelves

Many house items that we use frequently or want to display are stored on shelves. Many times, the shelves are strictly utilitarian, using otherwise wasted space in a closet or kitchen cabinet. Other times, they are part of the decor, as pleasant to the eye as what they hold. The latter type are fun projects—projects for giving to others or yourself.

Modular Units

One way to construct attractive shelves without ignoring practical function is to think of modular units that can be placed together to suit a particular purpose, space, or decor. That is a major advantage of the idea; being free at any time to rearrange the units to accommodate changes in storage or display items or merely to provide a change of scene.

Two units, made in some quantity, comprise the entire shelf project that is shown in FIG. 5-1. All of them do not have to be made in an evening or over a weekend, but constructing a few hours at a time will soon produce enough components to cover a wall.

The sizes of the modules (which are just simple boxes) made for the project are shown in FIG. 5-2. You can make changes as long as one is half the size of the other. Use solid softwood or hardwood lumber of your choice and opt for joints that you can accomplish with minimum fuss. Butt joints, rabbet joints, and miters will do. Fasteners can be finishing nails that are set and concealed with wood dough, or screws that are driven in counterbored holes and concealed with plugs.

Fig. 5-1. *Modular units can be made in small or large quantities to suit a space or an application. Since the units are not attached, they can be rearranged at any time.*

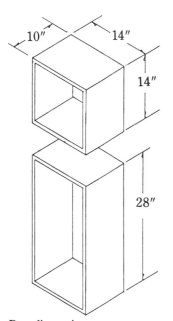

Box dimensions

Fig. 5-2. *These are the module dimensions used for the book project. There can be changes but one unit must be half the size of the other.*

Plywood is another option, again using joints of your choice. Edges, however, will have to be concealed but this is not difficult to do with modern wood-veneer edging that is applied with a household pressing iron.

The boxes can be left open or you can add thin backs by nailing them on. For a more professional look, inset them in grooves cut into the other components. These ideas are sketched in FIG. 5-3.

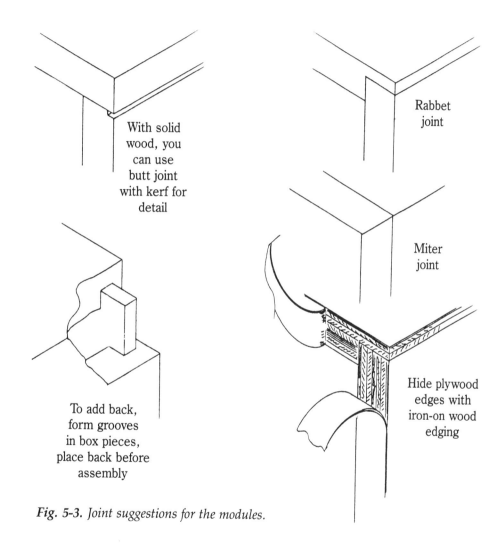

With solid wood, you can use butt joint with kerf for detail

Rabbet joint

Miter joint

To add back, form grooves in box pieces, place back before assembly

Hide plywood edges with iron-on wood edging

Fig. 5-3. Joint suggestions for the modules.

Combine creativity and practicality when previewing what the final project will look like. The modules do not have to be used alone. Spanning across them with boards or adding a slab for a desk top or including interior crosspieces can make them serve different purposes (FIG. 5-4).

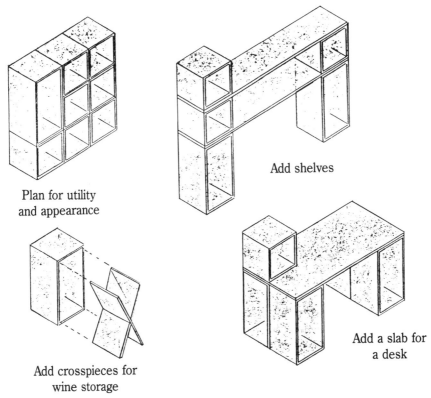

Plan for utility
and appearance

Add shelves

Add crosspieces for
wine storage

Add a slab for
a desk

Fig. 5-4. These sketches show some alternate ways in which the modules can be utilized.

Wall Shelf

A wall shelf should be attractive and well made but not overly embellished since it should perform mainly as a backdrop for the items that are on display. The project in FIG. 5-5 was designed with those thoughts in mind. Study the assembly drawing in FIG. 5-6 and TABLE 5-1 for material requirements before starting work. Use a clear softwood if you plan to paint the project, a hardwood if you are staining or are using clear finish.

Start by cutting two pieces for the sides (#1) to overall size and, on inside faces, mark the locations of the dadoes. You will be sure of alignment if you butt the pieces and draw the dado lines across both of them. Cut the dadoes by, preferably, working on a table saw or radial-arm saw. Make test cuts in scrap stock to check accuracy before cutting the good material. Tape the pieces together face-to-face so the profile on the front edge can be cut on both at the same time. Since the combined pieces are 1 1/2 inches thick, the sawing is a feasible job for a scroll saw.

Cut the remaining parts to size and put shelves and sides together, dry, using bar clamps to hold them. Drill two holes through the sides into each shelf for #6

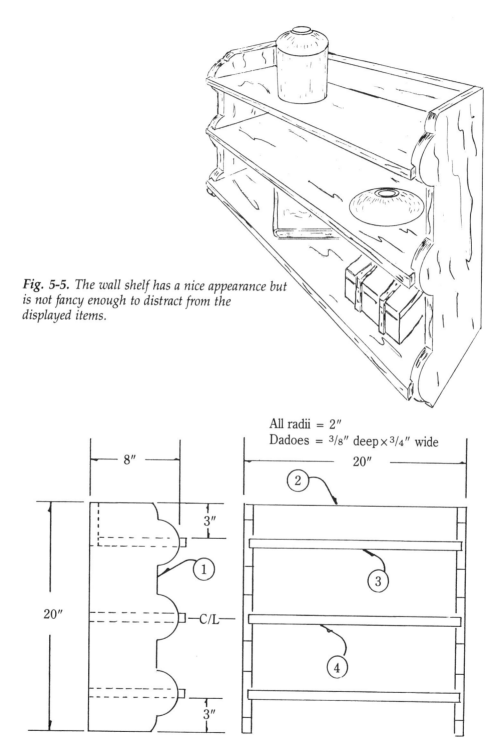

Fig. 5-5. *The wall shelf has a nice appearance but is not fancy enough to distract from the displayed items.*

All radii = 2″
Dadoes = $^{3}/_{8}$″ deep × $^{3}/_{4}$″ wide

8″

20″

3″

①

20″

—C/L—

②

③

④

3″

Fig. 5-6. *Assembly details of the wall shelf.*

Table 5-1. Materials List.

Req'd	Part No.	Size
2	1	$3/4'' \times 8'' \times 20''$
1	2	$3/4'' \times 33/4'' \times 181/2''$
1	3	$3/4'' \times 73/4'' \times 191/4''$
2	4	$3/4'' \times 81/2'' \times 191/4''$

$1\frac{1}{2}$-inch flat-head screws. Counterbore the holes but no more than about $1/16$ inch since the material left after dadoing is only $3/8$ inch. Separate the pieces and after cleaning away the chips that are left by drilling, reassemble them, this time with glue and screws. Follow the same procedure to install the top, back component (#2).

Use wooden plugs to fill the counterbored holes, seating them with a drop of glue and sanding them flush after the glue dries. Buttons can be used instead of plugs to add decorative detail.

The project is wide enough so it can be secured to a wall with two screws through the top piece that penetrate wall studs. Remember that wall studs are 16 inches on centers. Use a level when you do the mounting to be sure the project will be horizontal.

Corner Shelves

Corner shelves are often used to fill a void in the decor of a room, or they are placed on a piece of furniture that is already in place to serve as a display unit for treasured keepsakes or even small plants.

The project shown in FIG. 5-7 is a typical corner-shelf design. There is a lot of latitude in the number and the sizes of the shelves. The project can be small if it must not be too prominent, or it can be a major focal point when it is made to run from floor to ceiling.

The shelves are quarter circles. Hold them together as a pad so the holes for the dowels can be drilled through all of them at the same time. Put the parts together, spacing the shelves as you prefer, and drive finishing nails through the back edges of the shelves and into the dowels. The materials you work with will determine the weight of the project—$1/2$-inch-thick shelves with $1/2$-inch dowels, $3/4$-inch shelves with $3/4$-inch, or 1-inch dowels, and so on. Much depends on the visual importance of the project and what you want to display.

Figure 5-8 shows the construction details for a similar project. The shelves are notched to receive square posts. There is a lot of latitude with this project, also, in terms of overall size. This might be the design to adopt for a floor-to-ceiling project since it has more visual stability.

The corner shelf in FIG. 5-9 is a typical design when the effect of the project is as important as what it will hold. Cut the two sides to overall size and join them as a pad before marking the shape on one piece (FIG. 5-10). Do the cutting on a

Fig. 5-7. *Corner shelf with quarter-circle shelves and heavy dowel posts.*

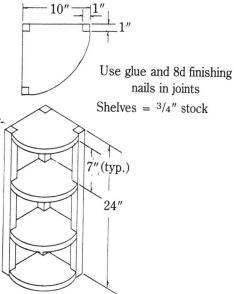

Fig. 5-8. *This corner shelf also has quarter-circle shelves but posts are square and set into notches cut into the shelves.*

10"   1"
1"

Use glue and 8d finishing nails in joints

Shelves = ³/₄″ stock

7″(typ.)

24″

Fig. 5-9. Corner shelves can be designed so they are just as important as what they display. This project has ''scrolled'' sides.

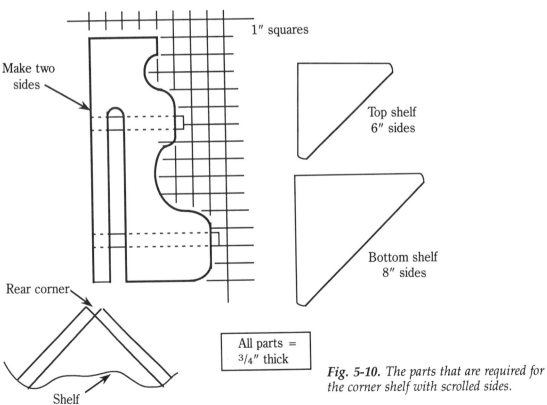

1" squares

Make two sides

Top shelf
6" sides

Bottom shelf
8" sides

Rear corner

Shelf

All parts =
3/4" thick

Fig. 5-10. The parts that are required for the corner shelf with scrolled sides.

scroll saw or bandsaw, or if necessary, with a heavy coping-saw blade. Assemble sides and shelves with glue and 6d finishing nails that you set below the surface of the wood and conceal with wood dough.

The book project was made of clear pine and stained with a light maple, but painting or using a hardwood and a clear finish are other options.

Shelf with Oriental Motif

The oriental shelf (FIG. 5-11) is typical of projects that must stand on their own and that enhance whatever items they display. Carefully study the assembly

Fig. 5-11. Display shelves can have a special motif, like this oriental design.

drawing in FIG. 5-12 and the material requirements in TABLE 5-2 before starting construction. Work with maple or birch if you plan a painted project; use something like teak if a natural finish will be more suitable.

Start with the hanger (#6); all other components can be fitted to it. Shape the piece on a power tool or by hand with a coping saw. Notice that the top has an opening to receive the link (#4). Sand all sawed edges to satiny smoothness. Cut the link to shape and hold it and the hanger together with a clamp while you carefully drill the hole for the 1/2 inch dowel (#5). Do not install the dowel at this time.

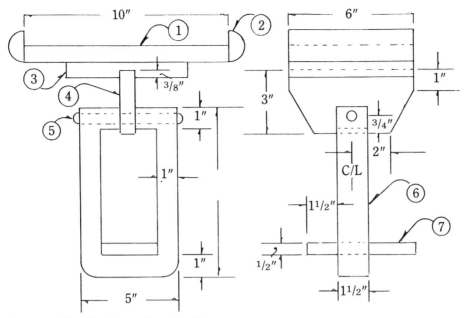

Fig. 5-12. *Details of the oriental shelf.*

Table 5-2. Materials List.

Req'd	Part No.	Size
1	1	$3/4'' \times 6'' \times 10''$
2	2	Half round—$6''$
1	3	$3/4'' \times 6'' \times 6''$
1	4	$3/4'' \times 3'' \times 6''$
1	5	$1/2''$ D. $\times 5^{1/2}''$
1	6	$1^{1/2}'' \times 5'' \times 8''$
1	7	$1/2'' \times 3'' \times 5^{1/4}''$

Shape the shoulder piece (#3) and dado it to receive the link. Assemble shoulder piece and link with glue and several 3d finishing nails. Since the nails will not be visible, it is not necessary to set them. Cut the shelf (#1) to size and attach the half-round molding (#2) to its ends with glue and 3d finishing nails. The nails should be set and concealed with wood dough.

Attach the shoulder piece/link assembly to the underside of the shelf with glue and 4d finishing nails that you set and conceal. Make the lower shelf (#7) and secure it in the hanger by coating mating areas with glue and keeping them together with a clamp until the glue dries.

The final step is to cut the dowel (#5) to length and to round off its ends before installing it. There are always finishing options but an appropriate one for this project would be to spray paint it with several coats of glossy, black lacquer.

6

For the Library

Bookcases are fine, of course, for storing quantities of books, but when you need to have a book close at hand or you want to display a special volume or two a different bookcase is needed. Ordinary bookends can be used but if the edition is special, it deserves an uncommon stand.

Book Ramp

Choose a hardwood to make the book ramp that is shown in FIG. 6-1 and detailed in FIG. 6-2. The sides can be cut individually or two pieces of stock can be padded so the two parts can be produced with a single sawing operation. The cut-out piece might be considered waste but it is large enough to be saved for future use.

Make the backplate, starting with a piece that measures $3/4$ inch × $2^1/4$ feet × $5^1/2$ inch. Drill the 1-inch hole and taper the sides so the back end measures 1 inch across. Round off the front end but leave the narrow end square. Assemble the sides and plate with glue and two 4d finishing nails into each edge. Wait for the glue to dry a bit and round off the back end of the assembly.

Provide a 5-inch length of 1-inch-diameter hardwood dowel and after you have glued it in place, cut its free end at an angle that will provide the slant of the project. This does not have to be precise since the tilt of the project is not critical.

Be sure that all parts of the project have been sanded satiny smooth and that the nails have been concealed with wood dough. Apply two coats of polyurethane varnish, sanding lightly between applications and again after the final one. Finish with a coating of paste wax.

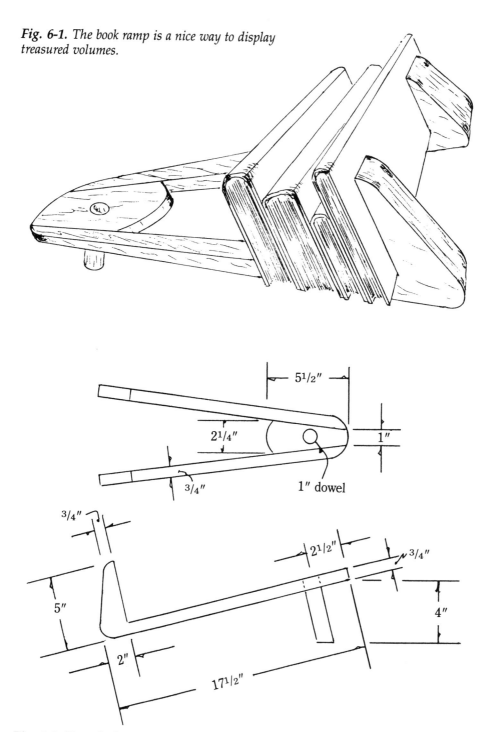

Fig. 6-1. *The book ramp is a nice way to display treasured volumes.*

5¹/₂″

2¹/₄″

1″

3/₄″

1″ dowel

3/₄″

2¹/₂″

3/₄″

5″

4″

2″

17¹/₂″

Fig. 6-2. *How the book ramp is made. Use a common or exotic hardwood for all components.*

Book Trough

The book trough (FIG. 6-3) is a quickie project. Make both ends (FIG. 6-4) with a single sawing operation by using the pad method. Be sure to drill the holes before you separate the pieces. Round off or chamfer the ends of the dowels before you install them. Coating the holes with glue should provide enough bonding to keep the dowels in place. If they fit loosely, toenail with 4d finishing nails at each connection point.

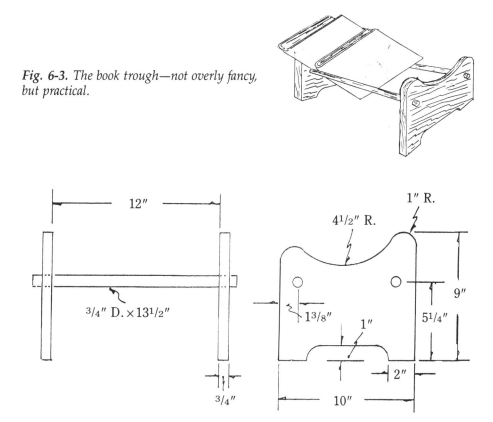

Fig. 6-3. *The book trough—not overly fancy, but practical.*

Fig. 6-4. *How the book trough is put together.*

Rustic Bookends

The rustic bookends (FIG. 6-5) have a unique appearance and can probably be made with either softwood or hardwood pieces that are salvaged from the waste bin. Strips of wood that are 1/2 inch or 3/4 inch thick and 3/4 inch wide are needed. The end strips should be about 7 inches long but intermediate ones should vary in height (FIG. 6-6).

Before assembling the strips with the diagonally placed crosspieces, rough up one surface and the edges with a rasp or by working with a drum sander. Put

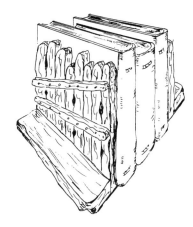

Fig. 6-5. The rustic "old fence" bookends.

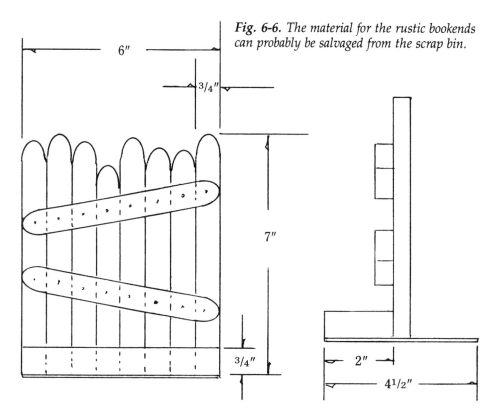

Fig. 6-6. The material for the rustic bookends can probably be salvaged from the scrap bin.

the parts together with a dab of glue at each contact point and add a ⁵/₈-inch or ³/₄-inch brad. Brass escutcheon pins instead of brads will add a decorative touch.

Cut the base to size and distress all areas but the bottom and the back edge. Attach the "fence" to the base with glue and 4d finishing nails. Add the aluminum sheet metal plate, which you can do with an epoxy. The plate is included so the first couple of books can rest on it and keep the bookends from moving.

Finish the project with stain if you want a particular tone and varnish, or use varnish alone for a clear finish.

Designing Bookends

The design of bookends can be as varied as the volumes they might hold. Although the basic structure is L-shaped, what you add to it can make it a distinctive gift. Some suggestions that can spark your creativity are sketched in FIG. 6-7. A letter will personalize a project whereas a cartoon character, that can be produced in quantity by using the pad-sawing technique on a scroll saw, will make the project more interesting to a child. The arrow is a popular version. Shape the arrow as a single piece, then cut it apart and glue the segments to the bookends so the arrow seems to pass through the books.

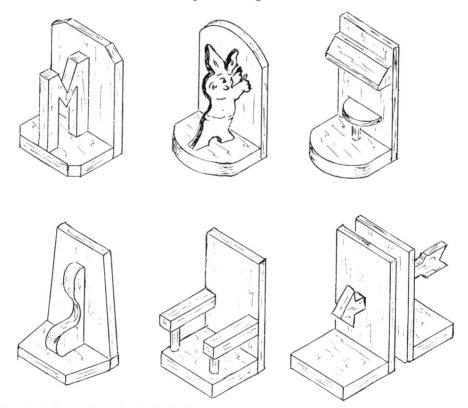

Fig. 6-7. Suggestions for bookend designs.

One problem with wooden bookends is that they lack the weight that is needed to support the books. One solution is to incorporate the metal plate that is part of the project that was shown in FIG. 6-6. Another way is to buy a few metal bookends and to attach your project to them using a few small, flat-head screws, or by bonding with an epoxy (FIG. 6-8).

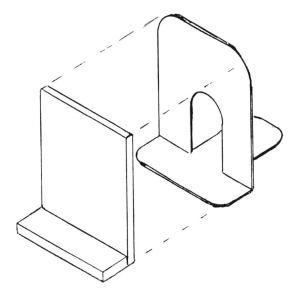

Fig. 6-8. Homemade bookends can be attached to commercial, metal ones.

A third method is to drill a few 3/8-inch or 1/2-inch holes through the base and to fill the holes with steel dowels that you conceal with wooden plugs. Work with a common or exotic hardwood. This seems appropriate for the projects and also contributes to the weight.

Lectern

Large tomes, like dictionaries and such, deserve some special attention. A lectern, like the one shown in FIG. 6-9, does the job while making the book easier to use.

Make the slab by gluing together three pieces of hardwood. A careful gluing job alone will suffice, but you can opt for using dowels in the connections. Cut the dadoes after the glue is dry and the slab has been cleaned and sanded. Form the tapered legs and install them with a glue joint. Attach the ledge, which can be the plain strips shown in the drawing (FIG. 6-10) or a suitable, small molding. This too should be installed with just glue.

Walnut or mahogany, finished with several applications of varnish, are good choices for this type of project.

Fig. 6-9. The lectern makes it more convenient to use large tomes like dictionaries.

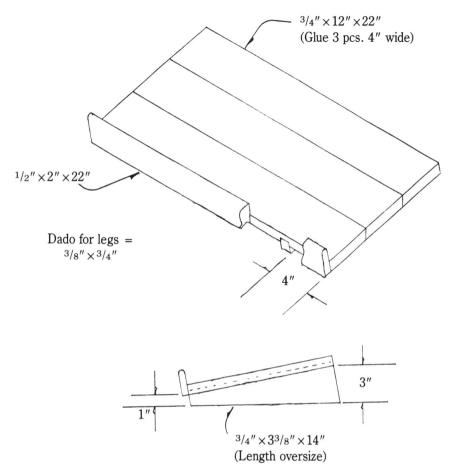

$3/4'' \times 12'' \times 22''$
(Glue 3 pcs. 4'' wide)

$1/2'' \times 2'' \times 22''$

Dado for legs =
$3/8'' \times 3/4''$

4''

3''

1''

$3/4'' \times 3^3/8'' \times 14''$
(Length oversize)

Fig. 6-10. *Construction details for the lectern. Check the size suggested here against the volume you make it for.*

7

Tables and Benches

Tables and benches are favorite woodshop projects. Any room in a home, including its outdoor areas, can use a table or a bench for eating, reading, or working. Projects of this type are almost multipurpose. A table can be used simply to display a favorite plant or to place current reading matter. The height of a table often tells its use—28 inches or 29 inches is right for dining, 17 inches or 18 inches is suitable for a coffee table, and about 25 inches or 26 inches is practical for a typewriter. Small benches become stools and are nice for a child to sit on, or to support feet when you stretch out to relax.

There is a lot of flexibility in project design. Even though plans are specific about shapes and sizes, you might see it with a different leg shape, a smaller or larger slab, or some particular embellishments that will make the project more suitable. In some cases dimensions can be increased overall so that, for example, a small bench or stool can be produced as a coffee table. The choice of material is a factor. A bench for indoor use might be made of pine or a hardwood. A worker might see it as a piece of patio furniture and make it of cedar or redwood so it would be more appropriate for the outdoors.

Basic Bench

The basic bench (FIG. 7-1) is typical of projects that can serve indoors or out, although our intent was to use it as a piece of patio furniture. Start the project by studying the assembly drawing in FIG. 7-2, and the material requirements that are listed in TABLE 7-1.

Fig. 7-1. The basic bench is furniture that can be used indoors or out. Suitable materials for outdoor use are redwood or cedar.

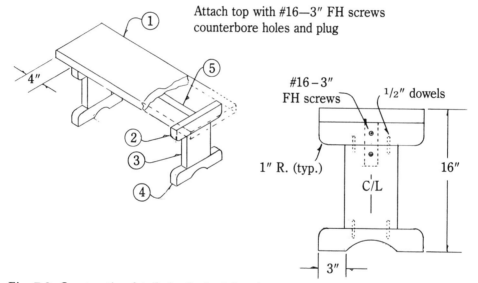

Attach top with #16—3″ FH screws counterbore holes and plug

4″

#16 – 3″
FH screws

1/2″ dowels

1″ R. (typ.)

C/L

16″

3″

Fig. 7-2. Construction details for the basic bench.

Table 7-1. Materials List.

Req'd	Part No.	Size
1	1	$1^{1}/_{2}″ \times 12″ \times 36″$
2	2	$1^{1}/_{2}″ \times 2^{1}/_{2}″ \times 12″$
2	3	$1^{1}/_{2}″ \times 6″ \times 9^{1}/_{2}″$
2	4	$1^{1}/_{2}″ \times 2^{1}/_{2}″ \times 12″$
1	5	$1^{1}/_{2}″ \times 5″ \times 25″$

Use waterproof glue all joints.

Make the top by ripping $1^1/_2$-inch stock to 4-inch width and gluing three pieces with the center piece that is placed so its annual rings oppose those of its neighbors. A well-done bonding job with waterproof glue will suffice, but if you like to reinforce edge-to-edge joints, include dowels in the connection.

Shape the parts that will be assembled as legs and drill into each of them for the dowels that will be used in the joints. One way to mark the parts for accurate drilling is to clamp the three pieces together with mating edges upward and on the same plane. Use a square to draw a line across all of them. Use a marking gauge to scribe a centerline on the edge of the parts. The intersection of the lines tells where to drill the holes.

Put the leg parts together with the dowels, glue, and keep the assemblies under clamps until the glue dries. Cut the stretcher (#5) to size and hold it and the legs together temporarily with bar clamps. Drill at each end for the two #16 3-inch screws, remove the clamps, and after cleaning away drill chips, assemble the parts permanently with glue and the screws. If you want, counterbore the holes and hide the screws with plugs. Lag screws, with washers under their heads can be substituted for the flat-head screws. The substitution will not be out of line especially if the project will be used outdoors.

The final step is to attach the top. Place it in position and secure it temporarily with clamps. Drill three #16 3-inch flat-head screws into each leg and after removing the clamps and cleaning away waste chips, do the permanent installation with glue and the screws. The screws can be concealed with plugs that are glued in counterbored holes or with buttons to add a decorative detail.

Low Bench or Tall Table

The project that is shown in FIG. 7-3 is typical of designs that can be altered to suit different purposes by changing the dimensions of the components. The first project is a low bench or stool.

Fig. 7-3. The low bench has a tusk-joint detail.

Figure 7-4 and TABLE 7-2 show how the project is assembled and the materials that are needed. The joint between the bottom rail and leg is reinforced with a tusk. Actually, you can get by without the tusk but it does add an interesting detail and shows a degree of craftsmanship.

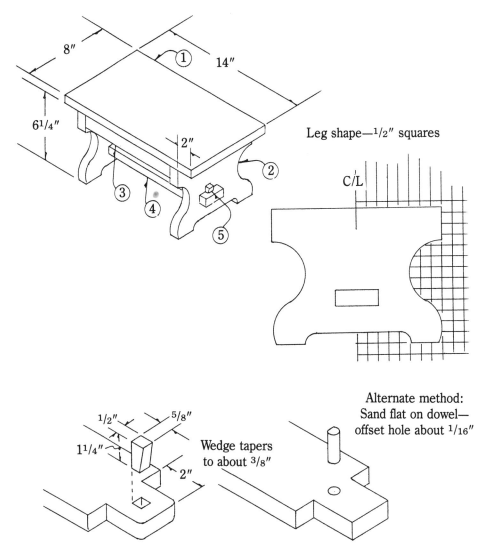

8"

14"

①

6 1/4"

2"

②

③

④

⑤

Leg shape—1/2" squares

C/L

Alternate method:
Sand flat on dowel—
offset hole about 1/16"

1/2"

5/8"

1 1/4"

2"

Wedge tapers
to about 3/8"

Fig. 7-4. How the low bench is made. Note the alternate method for the tusk. A hole is easier to form than a square opening.

The legs can be made of single pieces of stock. Since they are only 3/4 inch thick, two pieces can be joined as a pad and sawed simultaneously on a scroll saw or bandsaw. The rectangular opening can be formed in various ways, the easiest being by piercing on a scroll saw. If you work with a coping saw or saber saw, drill 1/4-inch holes at the corners and use the saw to cut from hole to hole. When the waste is removed, use a file to square the corners. In either case, stay a bit away from the layout line when sawing. The opening can be finished with a

Table 7-2. Materials List.

Req'd	Part No.	Size
1	1	$3/4'' \times 8'' \times 14''$
2	2	$3/4'' \times 6^{1}/4'' \times 8''$
2	3	$3/4'' \times 1'' \times 8^{1}/2''$
1	4	$3/4'' \times 4'' \times 14''$
2	5	See detail

file or with sandpaper that is wrapped around a wooden block. The point is, the opening should have straight edges and square corners and it should provide a nice fit for the rail that will pass through it.

The next phase is to cut the rail (#4) to length and to shape its ends as shown in the drawing. The distance from the shoulders of the projections must equal the length of the top rails (#3), which is $8^{1}/2$ inches.

Cut the top rails to size and assemble all the parts, but only with clamps. This is done so you can accurately mark the location of the opening that is required for the tusk. Remove the clamps and form the opening for the tusk, preferably with a mortising chisel. If this cannot be done, drill a hole and square it with a file, or leave the hole as is and use the alternate method that is detailed in the drawing.

With the lower rail installed, coat the mating areas of the top rails and the legs with glue and hold the parts together with clamps while you drive two 6d finishing nails through the legs into the top rails. You can see why being precise when making the lower rail is important. After the aforementioned assembly, the rail cannot be removed should it need attention.

Size and install the top with glue and several 6d finishing nails into each leg. The tusk is simply tapped into place. Set all nails below the surface of the wood and hide them with wood dough before you do final sanding and finishing.

The idea for using the same design as a tall table is shown in FIG. 7-5. Since the top is a much broader slab, it should be made of several pieces of wood. The pieces can be joined simply or in more advanced fashion by including dowels and endboards that are joined to the assembly with blind splines. This assembly design is appropriate for this type of table.

The legs, being 20 inches wide, are fashioned from two pieces. Pad the half pieces so you can cut the profile on both at the same time. Also, form half of the rectangular opening for the bottom rail before you separate the parts. Use glue and dowels when you connect them.

Make the rails and follow the same assembly procedure that was described for the low bench. In this case use flat-head screws as fasteners, setting them in counterbored holes and concealing them with wooden plugs made of the same material used for the project. If you would like the table to have a more substantial appearance, use $1^{1}/2$-inch stock instead of $3/4$ inch.

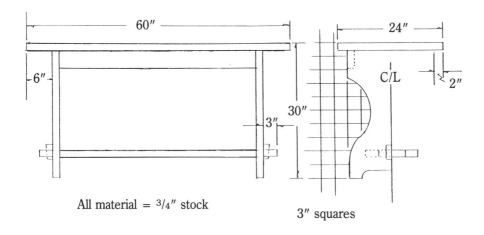

All material = 3/4" stock

3" squares

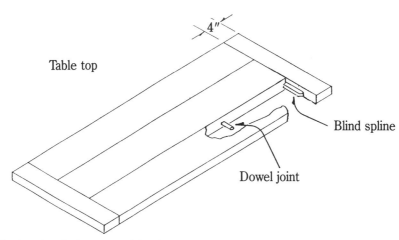

Table top

Blind spline

Dowel joint

Fig. 7-5. The low bench design used for the construction of a tall table.

Small Coffee Table

The top of the coffee table (FIGS. 7-6 and 7-7) can be a slab of plywood or it can be made of solid wood by joining several pieces edge-to-edge. If plywood is used, conceal its edges with wood veneer or with strips of wood or molding.

Cut the four brackets (#3 in TABLE 7-3) and bevel the two edges that will be visible when the parts are assembled. Mark the location of the leg holes on the top and use clamps to temporarily hold the brackets in place. This is done so you will be sure of alignment when you bore the holes. Mark each bracket and its corner of the top so it will be returned to the place it occupied when it was drilled.

Clean away any chips that were caused by drilling and attach the brackets with glue and a couple of #10 1 1/4-inch flat-head screws. When you do this, have

Fig. 7-6. The small coffee table uses large dowels as legs.

Table 7-3. Materials List.

Req'd	Part No.	Size
1	1	$3/4'' \times 12'' \times 18''$
4	2	$13/4'' \text{ D.} \times 143/4''$
4	3	$3/4'' \times 4'' \times 4''$

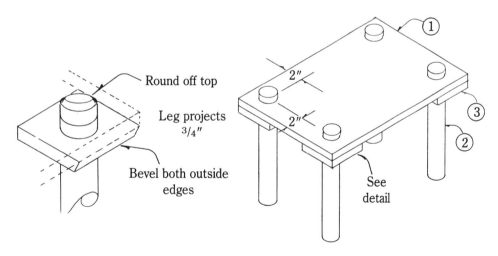

Fig. 7-7. Construction details of the coffee table. The brackets guard against wobbly legs.

a short piece of the leg material in place to ensure that the holes in the top and the brackets will fit together.

Cut the legs to length and chamfer or round off the top ends. Coat the walls of the holes with glue and insert the legs. Wipe off the glue that will spread to where you don't want it with a cloth dampened just a bit with warm water.

Allow the glue to set a bit, then toenail on the underside through each bracket and leg with two 4d finishing nails. You can use screws instead of nails.

Five-Board Bench

Our bench (FIG. 7-8) adopts the five-component concept that is found on many examples of Early American and Shaker furniture. The projects were straightforward; practicality and available materials are the prime movers. The book project is not a replica, and it does not have the austere ambience of originals.

Fig. 7-8. The five-board concept is a traditional design. Here it is used on a small bench.

Make the legs first, cutting them to overall size and marking them for the cut-out that is shown in the drawing (FIG. 7-9). Since the pieces are $1^1/2$ inches thick, it is not likely that they can be held together and sawed at the same time unless a bandsaw is available. In any event, doing the shaping will be easier if it is started by boring a 2-inch hole to provide the top radius.

Cut the two rails and form a $^3/8$-inch-$\times$-$1^1/2$-inch rabbet at each end. Attach the rails to the legs with glue and two 6d finishing nails at each connection. Cut the top to size and hold it in place temporarily with clamps while you drill and counterbore for the four #12 2-inch flat-head screws. Remove the top so you can clean away any chips that are caused by drilling and install it permanently with

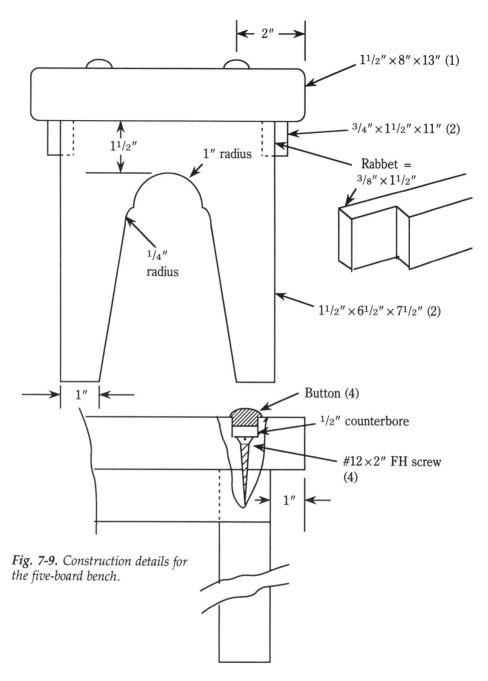

$1\frac{1}{2}'' \times 8'' \times 13''$ (1)

2"

$1\frac{1}{2}''$

1" radius

$\frac{3}{4}'' \times 1\frac{1}{2}'' \times 11''$ (2)

Rabbet = $\frac{3}{8}'' \times 1\frac{1}{2}''$

$\frac{1}{4}''$ radius

$1\frac{1}{2}'' \times 6\frac{1}{2}'' \times 7\frac{1}{2}''$ (2)

1"

Button (4)

$\frac{1}{2}''$ counterbore

#12 × 2" FH screw (4)

1"

Fig. 7-9. Construction details for the five-board bench.

glue and the four screws. Concealing the screws with buttons adds a nice touch.

Round off all edges and corners by working with a rasp or coarse file and work with sandpaper until all surfaces and edges are glass smooth. Finish with several coats of sealer and a final buffing with paste wax.

Distressed Bench

This project (FIG. 7-10) is similar to the five-board bench but is designed with dowels instead of routine rails. It is also different because of the way components are treated to look aged and rough-hewn before they are assembled. Figure 7-11 has construction details.

Fig. 7-10. The distressed bench is fun to make. You don't have to worry about marring the wood as you work. A blemish or two just adds to the effect.

Although you might not be able to produce the legs simultaneously by pad sawing because of thickness, you should, after they are shaped, hold them together while you drill the holes for the dowels. Cut the top to size and do some distressing before you begin assembly. Distressing consists of using a rasp to round off all edges and corners in a random way. Surfaces are antiqued by denting them lightly in an irregular pattern with a small hammer. Another way is to whack the surfaces with a length of chain.

Assemble the legs and dowel with glue and by toenailing at inside connection points with a single 4d finishing nail. Hold the top in place temporarily while you drill and counterbore for the six #14 $2^1/4$-inch screws. Attach permanently, after cleaning away debris, with glue and screws and conceal the screws with wooden plugs. Distress the plugs a bit so they will conform with the appearance of the top.

Work with sandpaper to remove any fibers that were raised by distressing and to achieve generally smooth surfaces. The book project was made of pine and toned with a maple stain. Apply stain generously and wipe off excess with a lintfree cloth. The stain will darken the wood more when dents occur but this

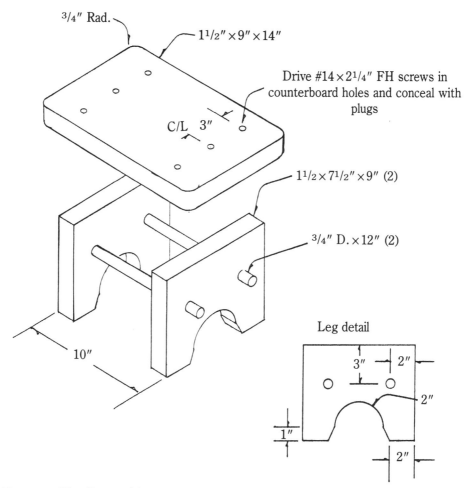

3/4" Rad.

1¹/₂" × 9" × 14"

Drive #14 × 2¹/₄" FH screws in counterboard holes and conceal with plugs

C/L 3"

1¹/₂ × 7¹/₂" × 9" (2)

3/4" D. × 12" (2)

10"

Leg detail

3" — 2"

2"

1"

2"

Fig. 7-11. *The distressed bench is assembled with dowels instead of conventional rails.*

will just add to the antique appearance of the project. Use a satin-finish varnish for final coats and rub all areas with fine steel wool.

Laminated Bench

The laminated bench that was shown in FIG. 7-12 has a distinctive appearance because its components are composed of separate pieces of contrasting wood. There are options—maple with cherry, teak with birch, or even something similar to pine with redwood.

The project is not as complicated as it might seem but you should study FIG. 7-13 to see how the parts are assembled, and check the material requirements that are listed in TABLE 7-4.

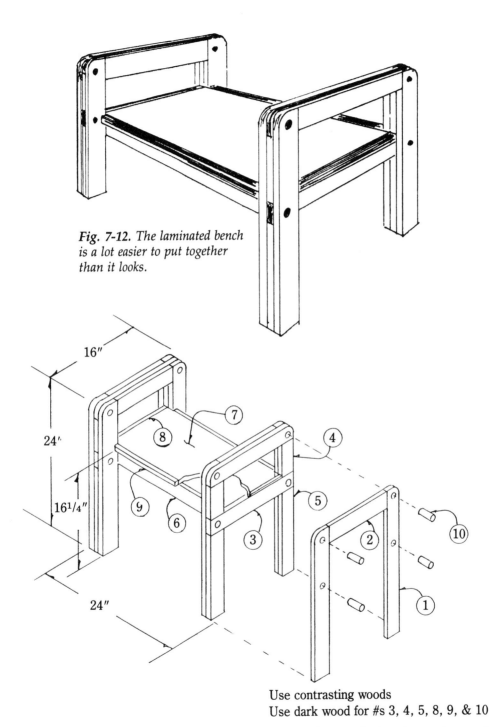

Fig. 7-12. *The laminated bench is a lot easier to put together than it looks.*

16"

24"

16¹/4"

24"

⑦

⑧

④

⑤

⑨

⑥

③

②

①

⑩

Use contrasting woods
Use dark wood for #s 3, 4, 5, 8, 9, & 10

Fig. 7-13. *Assembly of the laminated bench. Contrasting wood gives it a unique and pleasant appearance.*

Table 7-4. Materials List.

Req'd	Part No.	Size
8	1	$3/4'' \times 2^1/2'' \times 24''$
4	2	$3/4'' \times 2^1/2'' \times 11''$
4	3	$3/4'' \times 2^1/2'' \times 16''$
4	4	$3/4'' \times 2^1/2'' \times 5^1/4''$
4	5	$3/4'' \times 2^1/2'' \times 13^3/4''$
2	6	$3/4'' \times 2^1/2'' \times 21''$
1	7	$3/4'' \times 11'' \times 21''$
2	8	$3/4'' \times 3/4'' \times 11''$
2	9	$3/4'' \times 3/4'' \times 19^1/2''$
8	10	$3/4''$ D. $\times 2^1/4''$

First, cut all the parts that are required for the leg assemblies. The parts will go together easily if you start by coating the mating areas of parts #1 and #2 with glue and holding them together with a clamp. These pieces form the basic frame for the legs. Once they are together, the remaining parts (#3, #4, #5) will settle into place. Do the assembly work with glue and clamps. You can add finishing nails, but there is so much glue area that additional fasteners are not necessary. Be sure that all glue that squeezes out of the joints is cleaned off with a cloth dampened with warm water. The last step for the legs is to drill holes and to install the dowel plugs. These are not really required for strength but do add detail.

Cut the two rails (#6) and connect them to the legs with glue and two #6 $1^1/2$-inch flat-head screws at each end. The screws are in a hidden area so you do not have to worry about concealing them with plugs.

Cut the seat (#7) to size and use glue and clamps to secure it to the rails. You can add several glue blocks underneath along each side, gluing them and toe-nailing to the rails and seat with 3d finishing nails.

Add the trim pieces (two each of #8 and #9). Check the length that is required for these parts by measuring the assembly to be sure they will fit snugly. Attach the trim with glue and 6d finishing nails that you set and conceal with wood dough.

Since the project is made with contrasting wood, about the only logical finish that would bring out the character and tones of the wood would be a satin-finish varnish. Apply a coat of sanding sealer first. Go over all parts with fine sandpaper when the sealer is dry and use a tack cloth or something similar, to remove sanding dust. Apply two coats of varnish with a light sanding between applications and after the final one.

Lamp Table

Is there a household that wouldn't welcome one or two bedside tables to hold a reading lamp and books? The example shown in FIG. 7-14 also includes a practical

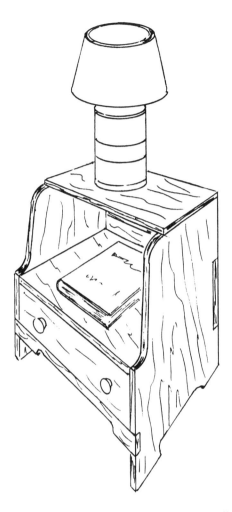

Fig. 7-14. *Lamp tables are nice to have by the bedside. This one provides room for books and a drawer to keep notions in.*

storage drawer. Since the project will have exposed edges, choose a cabinet-grade, lumber-core plywood as the material.

Figure 7-15 shows the components and illustrates how they are assembled. Check TABLE 7-5 for the sizes of the parts that are needed.

Start by cutting two pieces for the sides and tacknailing them together in waste areas so they can be shaped simultaneously. Cutting involves the recess at the base, the curved front, and the notches that are needed for the front rail and the back (parts #3 and #4). Follow by cutting and shaping the front rail, and cutting the back and the top (#2) to size.

At this point, you can start assembling by connecting the top, sides, and rail. Use glue in all joints but decide whether fasteners should be finishing nails that are set and hidden with wood dough, or screws hidden with wooden plugs. The latter method takes more time and care but seems more appropriate for this type of project. If you use screws, choose #6 1^1/2 inch; finishing nails can be 6d.

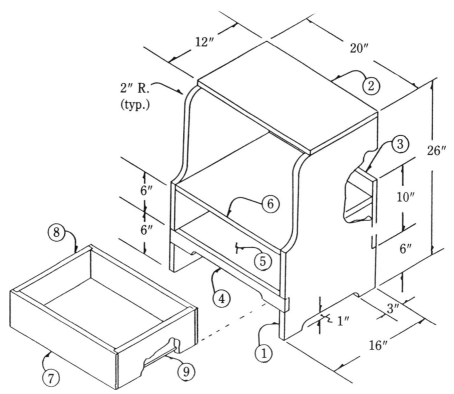

Fig. 7-15. *Assembly of the lamp table. The drawer design is very basic but you can use more sophisticated joints if you wish.*

Table 7-5. Materials List.

Req'd	Part No.	Size
2	1	$3/4'' \times 16'' \times 26''$
1	2	$3/4'' \times 12'' \times 20''$
1	3	$3/4'' \times 10'' \times 20''$
1	4	$3/4'' \times 2'' \times 20''$
1	5	$3/4'' \times 14^{1}/_{2}'' \times 18^{1}/_{2}''$
1	6	$3/4'' \times 15^{1}/_{4}'' \times 18^{1}/_{2}''$
2	7	$3/4'' \times 6'' \times 18^{1}/_{2}$
2	8	$3/4'' \times 6'' \times 14^{1}/_{2}''$
1	9	$1/4'' \times 14^{1}/_{4}'' \times 17^{3}/_{4}''$

Also need two readymade drawer pulls; drawer bottom set into $1/4''$ wide $\times$ $3/8''$ deep grooves cut into four parts of drawer. Assemble parts with glue and 6d finishing nails, set and conceal with wood dough.

Make and install the shelves (#5 and #6). Measure the assembly before cutting the shelves to be sure they will fit correctly. The case is finished when you have cut and installed the back.

Cut parts for the sides and front and back of the drawer. Check against what you have assembled so far to be sure the drawer will slide easily. The front and back of the drawer have 3/8-inch-×-3/4-inch rabbets cut at each end. The next step is to form the 1/4-inch-wide-×-3/8-inch-deep groove for the bottom in all four drawer pieces. Put the parts together using glue and fasteners at the rabbet joints; do not glue in the bottom. This is typical of drawer construction since movement that might be caused by atmospheric conditions should be allowed for.

You can make a couple of drawer pulls but it is easier to buy them, especially since there is such an abundance of different materials, shapes, and sizes.

The drawer construction and method of installation is not the most advanced. Readers who would like to do more can, for example, substitute dovetails for rabbet joints, and have the drawer slide on guides instead of the shelf. Readymade metal-drawer slides can also be used.

End Table

The end table shown in FIG. 7-16 was designed with an informal look. The ambience will, of course, be determined in part by the materials that are used. Stained

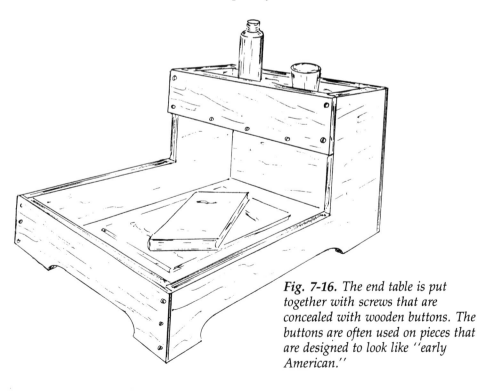

Fig. 7-16. The end table is put together with screws that are concealed with wooden buttons. The buttons are often used on pieces that are designed to look like ''early American.''

pine is on the homey side, whereas walnut or mahogany have a more formal appeal. Whatever your choice, work with cabinet-grade, lumber-core plywood.

Check the assembly drawing (FIG. 7-17) and the materials list in TABLE 7-6 before starting work.

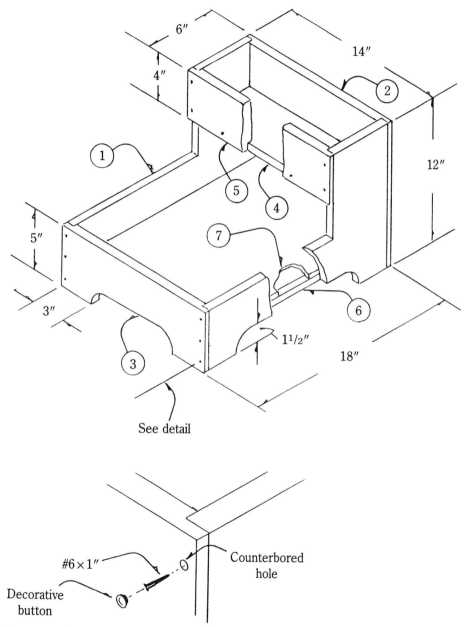

Fig. 7-17. *Construction details of the end table. You can choose to use plugs, sanded flush, or decorative buttons to conceal the screws.*

Table 7-6. Materials List.

Req'd	Part No.	Size
2	1	$3/4'' \times 12'' \times 17^{1}/_{4}''$
1	2	$3/4'' \times 12'' \times 14''$
1	3	$3/4'' \times 5'' \times 14''$
1	4	$3/4'' \times 47/8'' \times 12^{1}/_{2}''$
1	5	$3/4'' \times 4'' \times 14''$
2	6	$1/2'' \times 1/2'' \times 16^{1}/_{2}''$
2	6	$1/2'' \times 1/2'' \times 12^{1}/_{2}''$
1	7	$1/4'' \times 12^{1}/_{2}'' \times 16^{1}/_{2}''$

Attach cleats (#6) with 3d nails, attach bottom (#7) with $3/4''$ brads, all rabbet cuts = $3/8''$ deep $\times$ $3/4''$ wide.

Make the two sides and install the two cleats (#6) that will support the bottom with glue and 5d box nails. Cut the front and the back, rabbeting both edges on each of them $3/4$ inch deep $\times$ $3/4$ inch wide. Connect these pieces to the sides with glue and #6 1-inch screws. Drive the screws into counterbored holes and conceal them with wood buttons. You can conceal the screws with plugs, sanded flush, but the buttons are more creative.

Make and install the bottom of the compartment (#4). Cut this piece after taking measurements from the assembly. Put the part in place with glue and hold it with a clamp until you make and install the front of the compartment (#5). Check the measurements of the assembly before you cut the component. Be aware that it requires a rabbet cut on both ends and along the bottom edge. Install the front with glue and #6 1-inch screws that you conceal with buttons. The reason for holding the bottom of the compartment in place with a clamp is to avoid having to drive fasteners through the sides.

Cut the bottom, again measuring before cutting. The bottom rests on the cleats and does not need more than glue to keep it in place.

Finishing depends on the material you chose and whether the project must fit a particular decor. Maple stain on pine, or a natural finish on walnut or mahogany are typical options.

For the Garden

Plants that are placed in a container acquire a particular character. They become prima donnas—favorites on display. A plant that has no distinction in the ground with others is suddenly on a pedestal. Containers are welcome gifts for friends and for yourself, and when planted, reciprocate for a long time with color and greenery. Many people, especially those with limited space, have become aware that containers can also be used to grow vegetables. We have planted produce like cucumbers and tomatoes and enjoyed right-from-the-vine salads.

Another aspect of container gardening is mobility; plants are easily moved to ensure proper climate, and should you move, that treasured specimen that you have nurtured for a long time can go along with you.

Although heart redwood and cedar are preferred materials for plant containers, just about any species can be used if it is treated to guard against rot and weather damage. Wood can be coated with preservatives that contain copper sulfate—Copper Green and Cuprinol are examples. Preservatives that contain pentachlorophenol should *not* be used since the product will always be toxic to plants.

Joints do not have to be fancy but it is a good idea to use waterproof glue in the connections. Any plywood that is used should be exterior grade. House-siding plywood, especially the textured varieties, are excellent choices. Use weather-resistant fasteners, galvanized or aluminum nails, screws made of stainless steel or brass, and so on.

The Basic Box

Any container can be visualized as an open box that is designed to withstand the effects of soil and moisture (FIG. 8-1). Drill holes through the bottom for drainage—more or less depending on the size of the container—and cover each hole with a square of aluminum screening. Seal inside seams with a bead of caulking. Always include feet in the design so the bottom of the container will not directly contact soil or concrete. This eliminates a rotting situation and allows excess water to flow out freely. On large containers, swivel-type casters can be substituted for wooden feet.

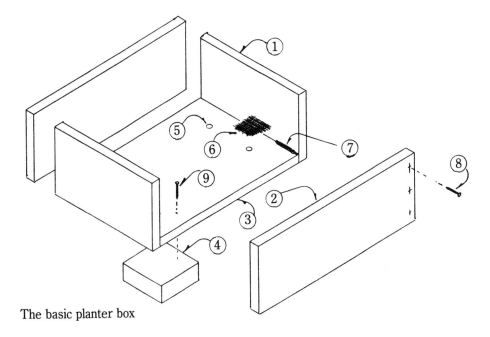

The basic planter box

    1. 2 ends—$3/4'' \times 6'' \times 10''$
    2. 2 sides—$3/4'' \times 6'' \times 16''$
    3. 1 bottom *—$3/4'' \times 10'' \times 14^{1}/_{2}''$
    4. 4 feet—$1^{1}/_{2}'' \times 4'' \times 4''$
    5. 4, $1/2''$ drainage holes
    6. Cover holes with aluminum screening
    7. Seams may be sealed with caulking
    8. Assemble components with 6d galvanized nails
    9. Attach feet with 7d galvanized nails **

    * Bottom can be pieces of $3/4''$ stock or a single piece of exterior grade plywood

    ** Waterproof glue may be used in the joints

Fig. 8-1. *The basic plant container is an open box that will stand up to the weather and that provides drainage for excess water.*

Although the basic box is a simple project that might be considered too pro-saic, there are many ways it can be treated or embellished so it will have more visual appeal. Some suggestions are offered in FIG. 8-2.

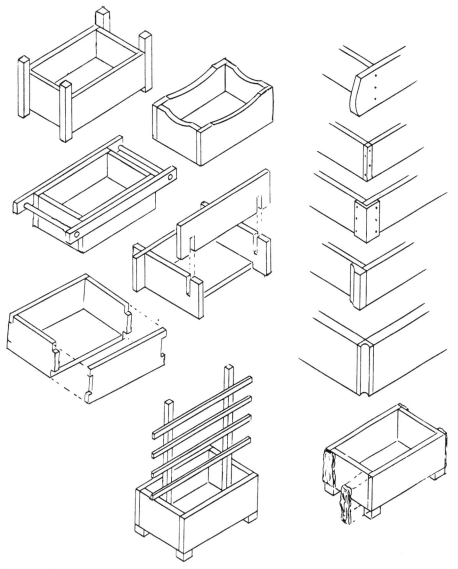

Fig. 8-2. Variations of the basic plant container. Connect all joints with waterproof glue and weather-resistant fasteners.

A simple box-type container is often incorporated in a fence or screen to break up the monotony of a line of blank boards (FIG. 8-3). This, of course, is planned for in advance. The frame for the fence includes two specially spaced posts and two headers that provide the opening for the container (FIG. 8-4).

Fig. 8-3. A simple open-box container can be incorporated in a fence or screen to break up the monotony of board after board.

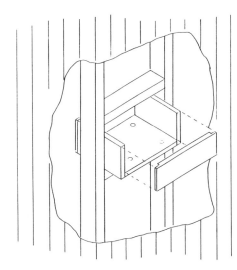

Fig. 8-4. Extra posts and headers provide the opening for a container in a fence or screen.

Small Container

Solid redwood lumber and ¼-inch-thick pieces of redwood siding are good materials for the plant container that is shown in FIG. 8-5. Notice in the construction drawing (FIG. 8-6) that a good deal of grooving is required, so it is best to consider the job as one for the table saw where the grooves can be cut easily and accurately. TABLE 8-1 lists the sizes of the parts that are required.

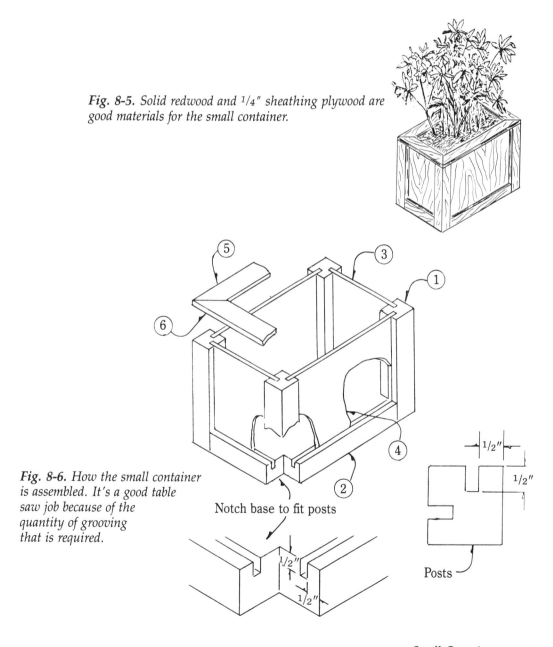

Fig. 8-5. *Solid redwood and ¼" sheathing plywood are good materials for the small container.*

Fig. 8-6. *How the small container is assembled. It's a good table saw job because of the quantity of grooving that is required.*

Notch base to fit posts

Posts

Table 8-1. Materials List.

Req'd	Part No.	Size
4	1	$1^{1}/_{2}'' \times 1^{1}/_{2}'' \times 8''$
1	2	$1^{1}/_{2}'' \times 8'' \times 12''$
2	3	$^{1}/_{4}'' \times 6'' \times 7''$
2	4	$^{1}/_{4}'' \times 6'' \times 10''$
2	5	$^{1}/_{2}'' \times 1^{1}/_{2}'' \times 8''$
2	6	$^{1}/_{2}'' \times 1^{1}/_{2}'' \times 12''$

Start by cutting the bottom (#2) to size and forming the grooves as shown in the drawing detail. Each corner of the bottom is notched to receive the $1^{1}/_{2}$-inch-square posts. Cut the posts to length, but before cutting the grooves, run a test on some scrap stock to ensure that they will align correctly with the grooves in the bottom. Assemble posts and bottom with glue and 8d box nails. Locate the nails so they do not enter any of the grooves. Since nailing area is confined, drill pilot holes before driving the nails.

Before cutting the panels (#3 and #4) to size, check the dimensions of the assembly to be sure the panels will fit correctly. Slip the panels into place without glue and cut the frame pieces (#5 and #6) to size. Apply glue to the top edges of the panels and posts before adding the frame. Drive two 6d box nails at the end of each frame piece into each post. The drawing does not show them, but use four pieces $1^{1}/_{2}$ inches $\times$ 2 inches $\times$ 2 inches as feet. Position the feet so they are away from the grooves and attach them with glue and 8d box nails.

Large Container

The container that is shown in FIG. 8-7 is suitable for a large plant or several small ones. By adding simple trellises, it will work fine for a climbing vine or even produce like cucumbers. Construction details are shown in FIG. 8-8; material needs are listed in TABLE 8-2.

Note there is a choice on how the corners can be made. Produce them by sawing 2×4s into an L-shape, or by joining two pieces of stock. Cut the panels (#1 and #2) to size and assemble them as an open box using glue and driving 5d nails through the end pieces into the edges of the sides. Attach the corners with glue and 3d nails.

Cut the bottom to size after checking the assembly to be sure of dimensions. Drill drainage holes through the bottom and put it into place with glue and 6d nails. Cut the frame pieces to size and put them into place after coating the top edges of the assembly with glue. Use 6d nails at each corner of the frame pieces and several between corners. The final step is to attach the feet with glue and 6d nails. The container, when filled with soil, will be heavy, so if you think you might want to move it about, substitute heavy, swivel-type casters for the wooden feet.

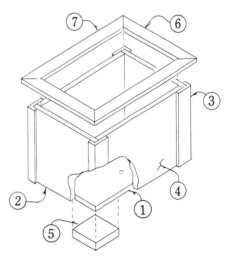

Fig. 8-7. Large container provides space for good-size plants. Use 3/4" × 1" strips of wood for ladder trellises.

Nails
Ends to sides—5d
Sides to bottom—6d
Feet—6d
Corners—3d
Frame—6d

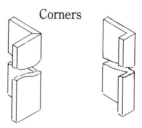

Corners

Fig. 8-8. The corners for the large container can be cut from solid wood or made by joining two pieces.

Shape from 2 × 4 or assemble
with 2 pieces of
1/2" × 2 1/2" × 16"

Table 8-2. Materials List.

Req'd	Part No.	Size
2	1	$5/8'' \times 16'' \times 24''$
2	2	$5/8'' \times 16'' \times 16''$
4	3	(See detail)
1	4	$3/4'' \times 14^{3}/4'' \times 24''$
4	5	$1^{1}/2'' \times 6'' \times 6''$
2	6	$3/4'' \times 2^{1}/2'' \times 20''$
2	7	$3/4'' \times 2^{1}/2'' \times 30''$

The High Rise

The high-rise container (FIG. 8-9) involves some intricate cutting, so like the small container we talked about earlier in this chapter, it should be done on a table

Fig. 8-9. The octagonal shape of the ''high rise'' gives it a distinctive appearance.

saw. Handtool workers should not ignore it, only that powersawing will make the job easier. Begin by checking FIG. 8-10 and TABLE 8-3.

Cut six pieces for the sides, being sure they are exactly 8 inches wide. Bevel the long edges on each of them to 30 degrees. Coat the beveled edges with glue and put the pieces together to form the hexagonal shape. Assembly will be easier if you can work with band clamps. If you lack the clamps, use some light cord, twisting it about the assembly with a strip of wood. The parts will hold together while you do the clamping if you start by stapling at the top and bottom of each joint.

Cut the bottom piece to the size that is suggested in TABLE 8-3 and rest the assembly on it. This way, you can mark the shape of the bottom so it will fit precisely. Drill 1/2-inch drainage holes and attach the bottom with glue and 5d nails. Make the corners (#2) from 2×4 stock and add them to the assembly with glue and 3d nails that you drive from the inside of the container.

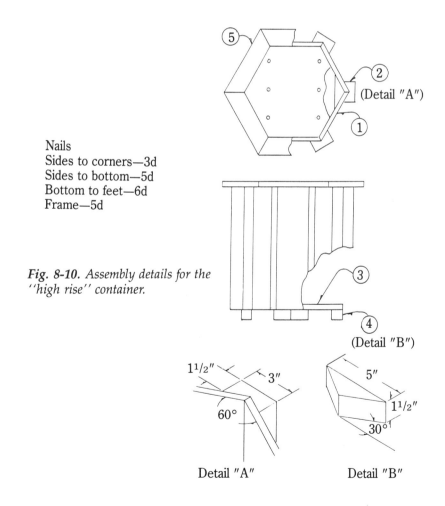

Nails
Sides to corners—3d
Sides to bottom—5d
Bottom to feet—6d
Frame—5d

Fig. 8-10. *Assembly details for the "high rise" container.*

Detail "A"

Detail "B"

Table 8-3. Materials List.

Req'd	Part No.	Size
6	1	$1/2'' \times 8'' \times 18''$
6	2	$11/2'' \times 3'' \times 18''$
1	3	$3/4'' \times 16'' \times 16''$ (oversize)
6	4	$11/2'' \times 11/2'' \times 5''$
6	5	$3/4'' \times 21/2'' \times 12''$ (oversize)

Cut the pieces for the top frame to overall size and check one piece on the assembly before cutting its ends to 30°. This piece can serve as a pattern for the others, or you can put it in place and cut the remaining in sequence to be sure of accurate fitting. The frame pieces are attached with glue and 5d nails.

The final step is to form the feet (FIG. 8-10B) and to add them with glue and 6d nails. Actually, the feet do not have to be shaped as the drawing suggests. Use square or rectangular pieces if you want to avoid the angular cutting.

The Cathedral

The *cathedral* is a whimsical name for the project shown in FIG. 8-11, but it was prompted by the domes that occur at each corner. The body of the container con-

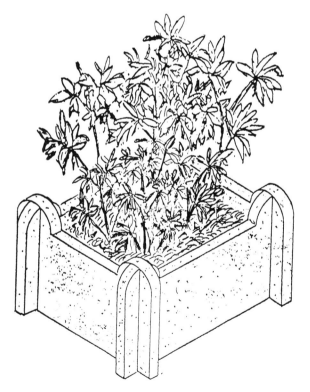

Fig. 8-11. The "cathedral."

sists of two each of the components shown in FIG. 8-12. The best procedure is to cut the parts to overall size and to form the slots before shaping the top edges. The work will go faster and parts will fit precisely if you use the pad-sawing method to form the duplicates. First drill a 3/4-inch hole where the slot ends. Straight-saw cuts will remove the waste, and a little work with a file will square out the corners.

Put the four pieces together with glue and use the assembly as a pattern to mark the size and shape of the bottom. Attach the bottom with glue and 5d nails and add the feet, again using glue and 5d nails.

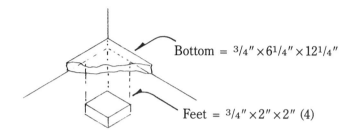

Bottom = $3/4'' \times 6^{1}/4'' \times 12^{1}/4''$

Feet = $3/4'' \times 2'' \times 2''$ (4)

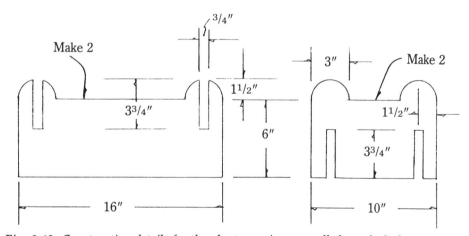

Fig. 8-12. Construction details for the plant container we call the cathedral.

Round Containers

You can produce round containers, like the one shown in FIG. 8-13, of just about any diameter by working with what is the *segment-cutting formula*. To determine the bevel angle of the parts (segments), divide 360° by their number and divide the result by 2 (FIG. 8-14). The first answer is the *joint* angle; the second answer is the *cut* angle. It does not matter how many segments you include or at what width, although the narrower the segments, the closer to a true circle you will come.

Fig. 8-13. You can make round containers by using the cutting formula that is explained in the text.

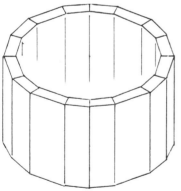

Fig. 8-14. The segment-cutting formula. The ''cut'' angle is always one half of the ''joint'' angle.

Formula to determine bevel angle—
divide 360° by number of parts,
then divide result by 2

   Coat the mating edges with glue and hold them together with staples at each end. Tighten the assembly with band clamps or with light cord that you twist with a strip of wood. Use the assembled segments as a pattern to mark the size and shape of the bottom.

Flower Pot Tree

Folks who like to display special plants in pots will find that the flower pot tree is a unique way to show them off (FIG. 8-15). The project is more appropriate for an outdoor location but if painted white or some other light color it will not be out of place in the corner of a room. Pine or redwood seem like appropriate materials but where you plan to place the project might influence your choice.

Fig. 8-15. The flower pot tree is a different way to display prized plants.

Cut the post to length and chamfer or just round off its top edge (FIG. 8-16, TABLE 8-4). Mark the location of the holes for part #3 and bore 1-inch holes through the post. Doing this on a drill press will ensure that the dowels will be horizontal when they are installed. Shape and attach the feet since this will make

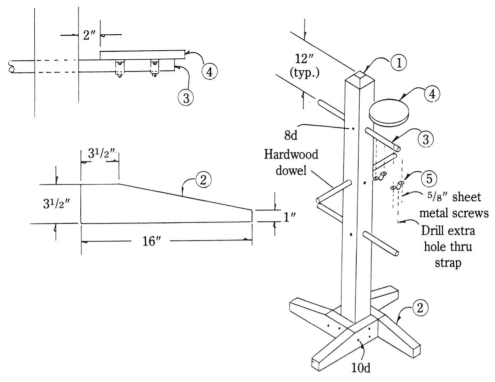

Fig. 8-16. Details for the flower pot tree.

Table 8-4. Materials List.

Req'd	Part No.	Size
1	1	$3^1/_2'' \times 3^1/_2'' \times 60''$
4	2	$1^1/_2'' \times 3^1/_2'' \times 16''$
3	3	$1''$ D. $\times 21^1/_2''$
6	4	$^3/_4'' \times 8''$ D.
12	5	Pipe straps

the remaining work easier to do. Attach the feet as shown in the drawing, using glue and 10d nails. Use box nails or work with finishing nails to conceal the fasteners.

Cut the 1-inch dowels to length and install them with glue and a single 8d nail that you drive through the side of the post. The platforms for the pots are circular pieces that can be produced more quickly if you pad-saw them. All six of them can be sawed at once if you have a bandsaw. Two at a time can be done on a scroll saw or with a saber saw, even with a coping saw that is equipped with a heavy blade.

The platforms are secured with straps that are normally used to secure plumbing. Note that the drawing suggests drilling an extra hole through the straps. This is so a third screw that passes through the dowel and into the platform can be used. The third screw is a safety factor to prevent the platform from tilting. Drill a pilot hole through the dowel for the screw to guard against splitting. Run a bead of glue on the top edge of the dowel before you install the platforms.

If you intend to give the project a permanent in-the-ground location, use a post that is longer by 18 inches to 24 inches and install it as shown in FIG. 8-17. The hole does not have to be more than about 6 inches in diameter. Set the post on a bed of gravel and fill around it with concrete. For this kind of work you can buy a ready-mix concrete by the bag; all you need to do is add water.

Fig. 8-17. This is the way to set the flower pot tree, or any post, in the ground. The hole should not be much greater than the size of the post.

18" – 24"

A-Frame

The A-frame project (FIG. 8-18) provides a means of displaying potted plants wherever they show best. One of the features of projects like this is that they provide a pleasant setting so the pots themselves do not have to be exotic; even prosaic clay pots will do.

Make the legs by following the pattern that is part of the assembly drawing (FIG. 8-19). TABLE 8-5 lists some of the parts oversized so there will be some leeway when cutting the parts to fit.

To make the legs accurately, start with one oversized piece that you shape at the top end and use as a pattern to mark the others. Put two parts together for each leg using glue and 7d nails and then clamp a straight board across the bottom end of the assembly as a guide for sawing the bottom angle.

Fig. 8-18. *The A-frame is an interesting way to display potted plants.*

Table 8-5. Materials List.

Req'd	Part No.	Size
4	1	$1^{1}/_{2}'' \times 3^{1}/_{2}'' \times 24$ (oversize)
4	2	$1^{1}/_{2}'' \times 4'' \times 7''$ (oversize)
2	3	$1^{1}/_{2}'' \times 2'' \times 9''$ (oversize)
1	4	$^{3}/_{4}'' \times 17'' \times 24''$
1	5	$^{3}/_{4}'' \times 17'' \times 14''$

Next, cut parts 2 and 3 oversized as suggested in TABLE 8-5, and add them to the legs with glue and 9d box nails. After the parts are in place, it will be easy to saw them to conform to the angles of the legs. The final operation is to saw the shelves (4 and 5) to size and to connect shelves and legs with glue and 7d box nails. In all cases, you can substitute finishing nails, or screws for the box nails if you want to conceal the fasteners.

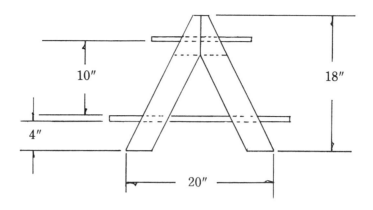

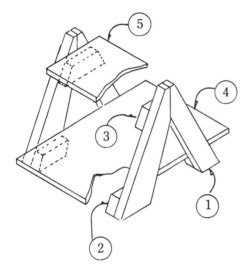

Fig. 8-19. How the A-frame is assembled.

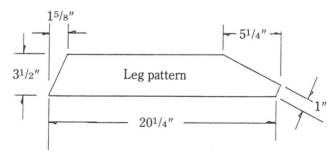

The Pedestal

The pedestal project (FIG. 8-20) is intended for displaying a prized ceramic pot and special plant. Use a lumber-core, cabinet-grade plywood for the legs and solid hardwood for the post. The legs (FIG. 8-21) can all be cut at the same time by pad-sawing if you can work on a bandsaw, or two at a time with other power tools, like a scroll saw or saber saw, or by hand with a coping saw.

Stay a bit outside of the layout lines when sawing and finish to the lines by working with sandpaper that is wrapped around a wooden block. Start with a coarse paper to remove the texture left by sawing and work through medium and fine paper until the edges are glass smooth. The easiest way to form the grooves in the post is with a dado assembly on a table saw. Chamfering the corners of the post is an optional feature.

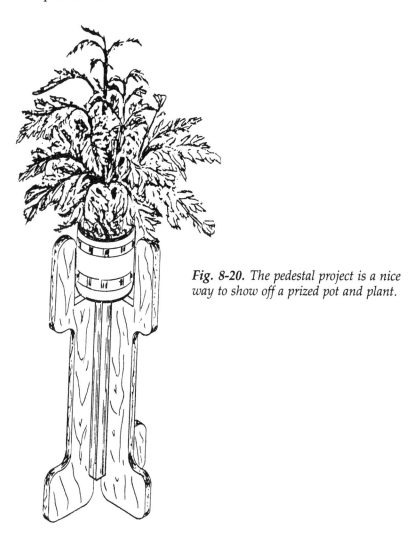

Fig. 8-20. The pedestal project is a nice way to show off a prized pot and plant.

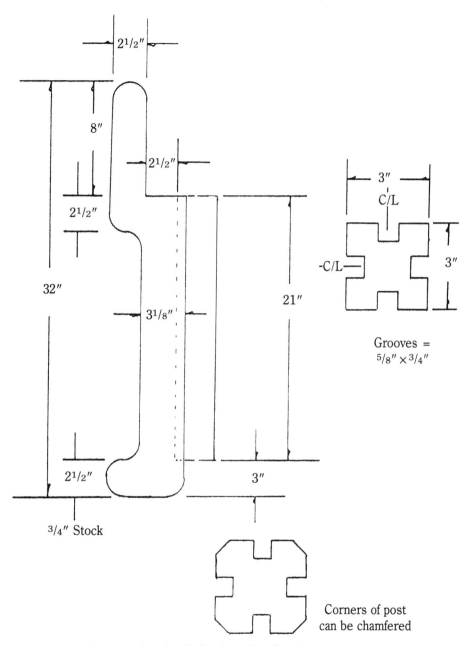

2½"

8"

2½"

2½"

32"

3⅛"

2½"

¾" Stock

2½"

21"

3"

3"

C/L

-C/L-

3"

Grooves =
⅝" × ¾"

Corners of post
can be chamfered

Fig. 8-21. Construction details for the pedestal project.

Coat all mating areas of the components with glue and secure the assembly with clamps until the glue dries. Remove any glue that squeezes out of the joints with a lintfree cloth that is dampened with warm water. Tone the project with stain if you want or just apply several coats of varnish.

Garden Tote

The garden tote (FIG. 8-22) is a prosaic project but it contributes in its own way to beauty by making it easy for the gardener to move about with the tools he or she needs. The removable handle is used to carry the tote but it also serves to form holes for planting seedlings or starting seeds. Pine or redwood are the best material choices.

Fig. 8-22. The garden tote is a practical accessory for a gardener. The handle is removable so it can be used to form holes for starting-plants or seeds.

Begin construction by forming the sides (FIG. 8-23). Pad two pieces of stock so the parts can be formed simultaneously. Cut the ends and the two partitions a bit wider than they should be so they can be sanded or planed to conform to the slope of the sides after they are installed. Cut the center bridge piece to size and after drilling the 3/4-inch hole, assemble all the parts using glue and 5d box nails. Use the assembly as a pattern for the length and width of the bottom and attach the bottom with glue and nails.

Cut the dowel for the handle to length and after tapering its end so it can penetrate soil easily, drill the two holes for the short dowels that will straddle the bridge. The dowels should fit nicely but not so tight that you cannot pull them out when you want to remove the handle.

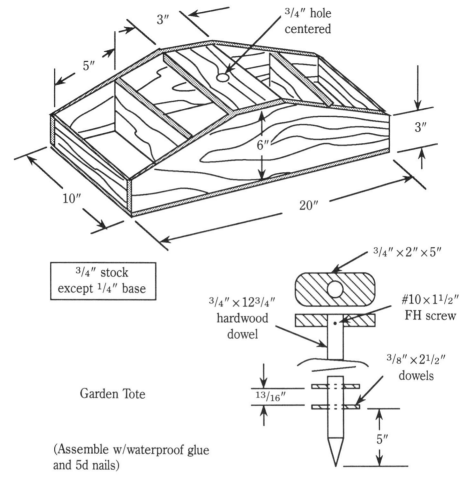

3" ← →
3/4" hole centered
5"
3"
6"
10"
20"

3/4" stock except 1/4" base

3/4" × 2" × 5"

3/4" × 12³/4" hardwood dowel

#10 × 1¹/2" FH screw

3/8" × 2¹/2" dowels

Garden Tote

13/16"

5"

(Assemble w/waterproof glue and 5d nails)

Fig. 8-23. Construction details for the garden tote.

Make the grip for the handle and attach it to the dowel with glue and a single #10 × 1¹/2-inch flat-head screw. Finish the project with several applications of an exterior-type sealer.

Duck Decor

The figure shown in FIG. 8-24 is a project that adds a whimsical touch to a garden area. Select the wood that you will use (pine, redwood, or cedar) and transfer the pattern in FIG. 8-25 to it. This is an ideal project for a scroll saw.

Round off all the edges and use sandpaper to smooth them. The project can be painted or protected with a clear finish. Add details with a felt-tip pen. The project can rest against some garden object or you can nail it to a sharpened dowel or strip of wood so it can be placed in the ground.

Fig. 8-24. Add a whimsical touch to the garden by displaying one or two duck figures. Add a 12"-16"-long round or square post if you wish to install it in the ground.

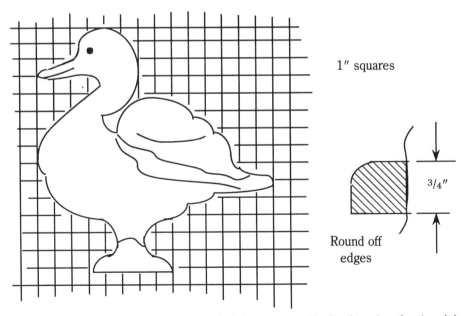

1" squares

3/4"

Round off
edges

Fig. 8-25. Pattern for the duck figure. Make it larger or smaller by changing the size of the squares.

Scroll Saw Projects

The first step when using a scroll saw (or "jigsaw") to make projects is to provide a pattern on the base stock that you can trace with a saw blade. Even straight lines, whether you move the work freehand or use a guide like a clamped-on fence, should be marked so you will have an ongoing check of whether the job is being done accurately.

The decision is whether to save the original. If not, the pattern can be applied directly to the wood with a spray of adhesive or rubber cement. If you wish to build a library of patterns, use carbon paper to transfer the pattern or make the pattern of cardboard, thin hardboard, or plywood so it will always be available as a template that you can trace.

A traditional method for duplicating patterns while retaining the model in original size is enlarging or reducing by using the squares method that is shown in FIG. 9-1. It is simple and allows an exact, larger or smaller reproduction, and you do not have to be an artist to accomplish it. Select a sheet of tracing paper that is larger than the illustration of the project and mark it with squares. Use the square sizes that are suggested or make them larger to increase the size of the project, or smaller to decrease it.

The next step is to mark the crucial points of the drawing at similar places on the squared sheet. Be generous with the number of points you mark, especially if the pattern is complex. The more marks you have, the easier it will be to connect them correctly. The system is something like those dotted children's pictures where the picture becomes live after the dots are connected.

A copying machine can be of tremendous help when you want to copy, reduce, or enlarge a drawing without damage to the original. Copying machine

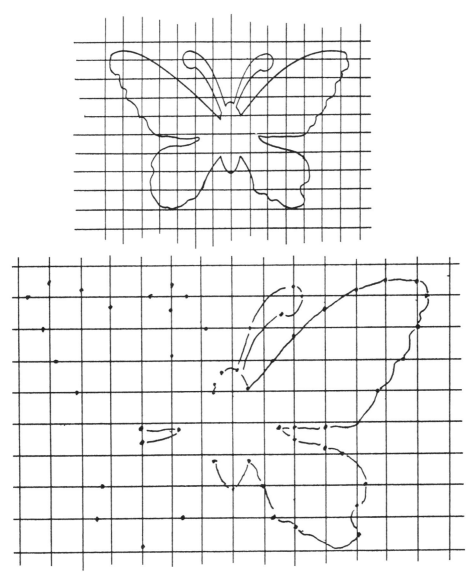

Fig. 9-1. *Patterns can be duplicated in larger or smaller sizes by using the squares method. For example, if the pattern has ¹/4″ squares and ¹/2″ squares are used for the duplicate, the working pattern will be twice the size of the original illustration. Of course, the reverse is true.*

establishments can be found most anywhere today and the cost of using them is pennies. An asset is that being able to easily make X number of copies allows you to be nonchalant about attaching one directly to the workpiece even though it will be destroyed during sawing.

Except for some accessory operations that some projects might need, such as drilling a hole or forming a groove in a base, all of the projects are scroll-saw ventures. If there are other tools in the shop and you choose to involve them in some way, why not? Smoothing sawed edges by using various size drum sanders in a drill press or portable drill is one example.

"Dennis the Menace" Project

As promised in the introduction, FIGS. 9-2 and 9-3 are patterns of Dennis the Menace, generously drawn for us by Mr. Hank Ketcham who created and keeps the

Fig. 9-2. The patterns for Dennis the Menace were drawn by Mr. Hank Ketcham, the creator of the famous cartoon character.

A variation
Paint Dennis with colors
shown on Sunday comic page.
H.K.

Fig. 9-3. *Mr. Ketcham suggests that Dennis be painted with colors shown on Sunday comic pages.*

famous cartoon character alive. The drawings do not suggest a size since the projects will be perfectly acceptable as small plaques for wall decor or as larger units that can partially cover a door.

Use 1/4-inch hardwood plywood for small plaques; 1/2-inch or 3/4-inch material for larger sizes. The plans show Dennis in a frame but you can eliminate it if you want to produce just the figure. Sand all surfaces and edges smooth and as Mr. Ketcham suggests, "Paint Dennis with colors shown on the Sunday comic page."

The Swan

The swan (FIG. 9-4) should have a delicate ambience so it might be best to make it in a small size, using a smooth-surface 1/4-inch hardwood plywood like maple or birch. If you use the 1/2-inch squares that are suggested, the size of the finished

Choose square-size to suit
$1/2'' \text{ squares } = 10'' \times 10 1/2''$

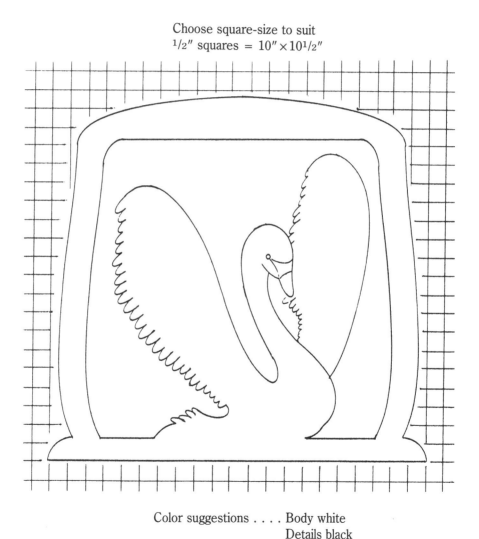

Color suggestions . . . . Body white
Details black
Beak brown

Fig. 9-4. The swan.

project will be about 10 inches×10¹/₂ inches. The project can be left natural, maybe with a coat or two of sealer, or painted in the tones that are suggested in the drawing. If you do color it, avoid anything like a heavy, glossy enamel. Pastels will be more suitable.

Floral

If you use the ¹/₄-inch squares that are suggested in the drawing (FIG. 9-5), the floral plaque will measure about 6 inches×9 inches. Like the swan, this project should have a delicate appearance so ¹/₄ inch or even thinner material is suggested. A thought for projects of this nature is to glue them on a ¹/₄-inch or ¹/₂-inch backing. This will make them sturdier, add depth, and, if the backing is painted a sky color, will give the flowers a more prominent aspect. The drawing lists colors to use for the flowers, but they are only suggestions. Actually, especially if you use a contrasting material for the backing, the project can be in natural tones.

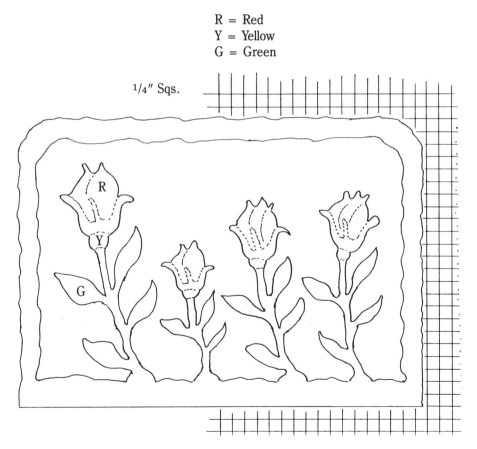

R = Red
Y = Yellow
G = Green

¹/₄″ Sqs.

Fig. 9-5. The floral.

Garden Rooster

If you use 1-inch squares for the rooster (FIG. 9-6), start with a piece of hardwood that measures about 11 inches×11 inches. Drill a 1/4-inch hole to represent the eye. Cut the base to size and drill the two blind holes for the dowels that allow the project to be placed in the ground. Coat the holes with waterproof glue before inserting the dowels. Attach the rooster to the base with glue and toenail with 3d finishing nails. Color the project with exterior paint or just apply several coats of exterior sealer.

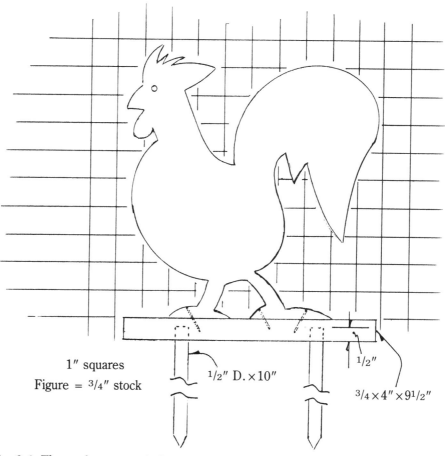

1" squares

Figure = 3/4" stock

1/2" D.×10"

1/2"

3/4×4"×9 1/2"

Fig. 9-6. The garden rooster is designed for ''planting'' in the ground.

Penguin Group

The reason for the penguin group (FIG. 9-7) is that it is whimsical and adds a light touch wherever displayed. Either softwood or hardwood can be used. Cut the base to size, using a similar or contrasting material, and chamfer its edges after forming the centered groove. Glue alone will be enough to secure the penguins

Base = 3/4" × 3"
Groove is 3/8" deep

1/2" squares

1/2" stock

Fig. 9-7. *The whimsical penguin group.*

to the base. Paint the entire project white and add details with a black, felt-tip pen.

Duck Parade

Start the duck parade project (FIG. 9-8) with a piece of 3/4-inch stock that measures 10 inches × 18 inches. An easy way to transfer the pattern is to make one

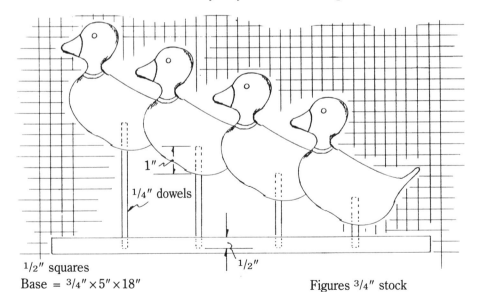

1"

1/4" dowels

1/2" squares

1/2"

Base = 3/4" × 5" × 18"

Figures 3/4" stock

Figures white, details black, beak and ring yellow

Fig. 9-8. *The duck parade. The figures are similar, so if you make one in cardboard it will be easy to trace the others.*

figure full size in cardboard. Use the cardboard as a template to mark the outline for the remaining figures. You will find it more convenient to drill the holes for the dowels accurately while the stock is in square form.

Use glue to secure the dowels in the figures and with the assembly on a flat surface, place a straightedge across the dowels so they can be sawed to end on the same plane. Make the base and hold the figures in position so you can mark the location of the holes. Coat the holes with glue and insert the dowels.

Wooden Cars

Wooden cars are popular toys for children and, if you are so inclined, are good products to offer for sale at local stores and fairs. Use a wood that will take some abuse, like 3/4-inch or 1 1/2-inch maple or birch. Do a good sanding job and round off corners with files and with sandpaper that is wrapped around a wooden block. Leaving the wood natural but protected with a coat or two of nontoxic sealer is a good way to finish.

The cars need wheels and they can be sawed out on the scroll saw but since four are needed for each project it is better to produce them in other ways. Hole saws or fly cutters will produce them quickly if a drill press is available or they can be sliced off from hardwood dowel or a cylinder turned in a lathe. Ready-made wheels are offered in many craftsman's catalogs. They come in various sizes and many are shaped for greater realism. It is not difficult to find some that have spokes or have circumferences treated to resemble tires.

Check FIGS. 9-9, 9-10, and 9-11 for the plans of four different cars.

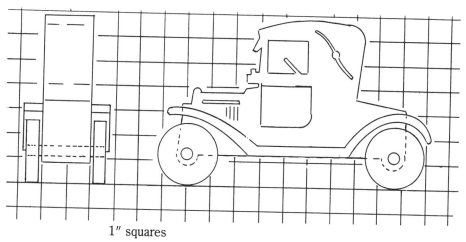

1" squares

Fenders and running board separate pieces glued on
3/8" axle loose in body, tight in wheels.
Paint or burn in details.

Fig. 9-9. The "flivver." The fenders are cut separately and then attached to the body with glue.

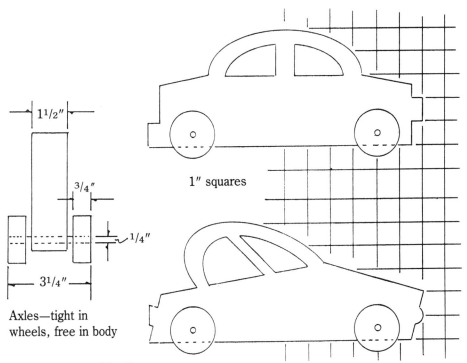

1½"

3/4"

1/4"

3¼"

Axles—tight in
wheels, free in body

1" squares

Fig. 9-10. Two "oldies."

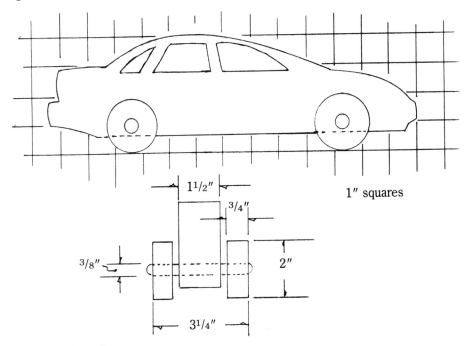

1" squares

1½"

3/4"

3/8"

2"

3¼"

Fig. 9-11. A modern car.

Animal Figures on Wheels

Animal figures are popular projects for scroll saws and when intended for children, become more intriguing when they are mounted on wheels. Since projects like this will inevitably be abused a bit, work with a hardwood like maple or birch. Sand all surfaces and edges satiny smooth and use a file and sandpaper on perimeters to eliminate sharp corners. Leave the wood naked or apply a coat or two of nontoxic sealer. The patterns that are offered in FIG. 9-12 are recognizable enough so they do not need details. Figure 9-13 shows methods to use for adding wheels. If you want to skip the drilling operations that are required for dowel axles, you can mount the wheels on #12×1³/₄-inch round-head screws. Place a washer between the wheel and the base of the project.

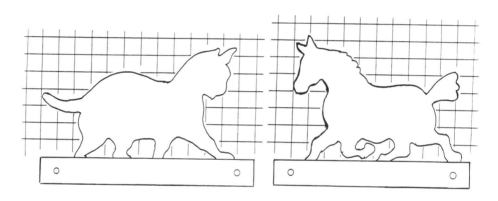

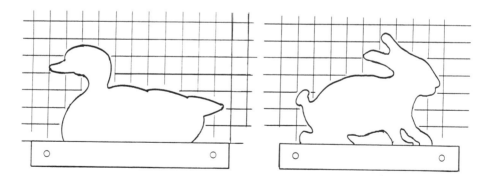

1″ squares

Use 1¹/₂″ hardwood for figures and base

Fig. 9-12. Animal figures on wheels.

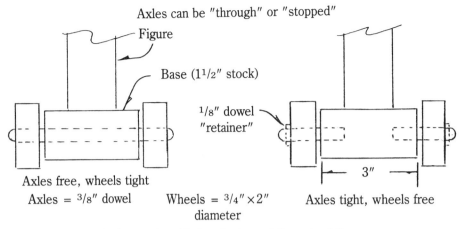

Axles can be "through" or "stopped"

Figure

Base (1½" stock)

⅛" dowel "retainer"

3"

Axles free, wheels tight

Axles = ³⁄₈" dowel

Wheels = ¾" × 2" diameter

Axles tight, wheels free

Fig. 9-13. *How wheels may be added to the base of the animal figures.*

½# Sqs.

Fig. 9-14. *The carousel. The text suggests how the project can be mounted on a base so it can be rotated.*

The Carousel

The carousel (FIG. 9-14) is a fun project to make and to give. If you use the 1/2-inch squares suggested in the drawing you will need a 3/4-inch-×-10-inch-×-12-inch piece of hardwood. The 3/4-inch thickness is suggested. Make an accessory for the project that consists of a 10-inch-diameter base with a central 1/2-inch dowel that extends above the base about 1 inch. Drill a 9/16-inch hole, about 3/4 inch deep in the base of the project so it can be turned when mounted on the dowel. When used this way, the project calls for colorful painting on both sides. Suggestions—green for the frame, red for the canopy. Paint the horse white, the blanket and harness red, and mane and eye black.

The project will serve as a nice wall decor when made of 1/4-inch-thick cabinet-grade plywood.

Key Rack

You might consider a key rack a rather prosaic project but it is a popular one and does fill a practical need. Our version is shown in FIG. 9-15. Choose a hardwood so the cup hooks for the keys will seat firmly. A natural finish is appropriate but you can add touches with kitchen-type decals that are available in stationery stores. Paint can be used to suit surrounding decor.

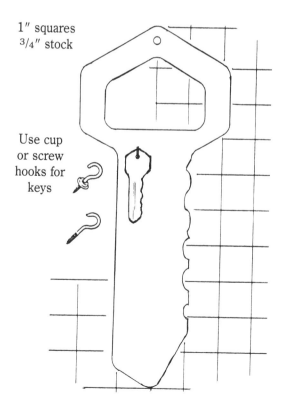

1″ squares
3/4″ stock

Use cup or screw hooks for keys

Fig. 9-15. The key rack is a classic scroll saw project.

Sundries

A couple of synonyms for sundries are "diverse" and "many." Some of the projects could logically have been placed in other sections since they are suitable for a particular environment. Others are adaptable and can serve where the builder or receiver chooses to use them.

Magazine Rack

The magazine rack in FIG. 10-1 is different from many conventional designs in that its partitions are formed by loops of a heavy cloth material. Start by cutting to overall size the eight pieces that will be assembled as two side frames (FIG. 10-2).

It will be easier to determine cutting angles if you draw a full-size profile of the frame on a sheet of paper. Position the parts and use a protractor to discover the angle. The angle can be set on a miter gauge if you are using a table saw or simply marked on the wood if you will saw by hand. A dado assembly on the power tool will make quick work of forming the half-lap joints. With a handsaw, you can choose between making two saw cuts or a single shoulder cut followed by chisel work to remove the waste. Round off the corners *after* you have assembled the parts with glue and 5/8-inch brads. If you would like to skip the angular sawing chore, just plan for vertical sides instead of slanted ones.

Hold the two assemblies together and drill the five 1/2-inch holes and the two 1-inch holes. Prepare five 1/2-inch and two 1-inch dowels, 12 inches long, and connect them and the frames after coating the inside of the holes with glue. Cut the dowels a bit longer than necessary and allow them to protrude when assembling. They can be sanded flush after the glue dries. The dowels will be more

Fig. 10-1. *The magazine rack uses canvas or duck or another heavy material of your choice as "partitions" for the reading matter.*

secure if you drive a single 6d finishing nail into them from the edge of the frame.

The project should have its finishing coats applied before the cloth material is added. The prototype was finished with the new Fleck Stone product that was described in chapter 3. Since the Fleck Stone supplies good coverage, the nail-heads did not need to be set. If you opt for a natural or stained finish, the fasteners should be concealed.

Use canvas or duck material, which is something like canvas but finer and lighter in weight, for the partitions. Start draping by securing the material under the first dowel with a few tacks or staples. Loop the material between dowels, securing at each crossing point with a tack or staple at each end (FIG. 10-2). About 80 inches of material, 10 inches wide, is required. Starting with cloth that is wider by a half inch or so and sewing hems on each edge will prevent the material from fraying.

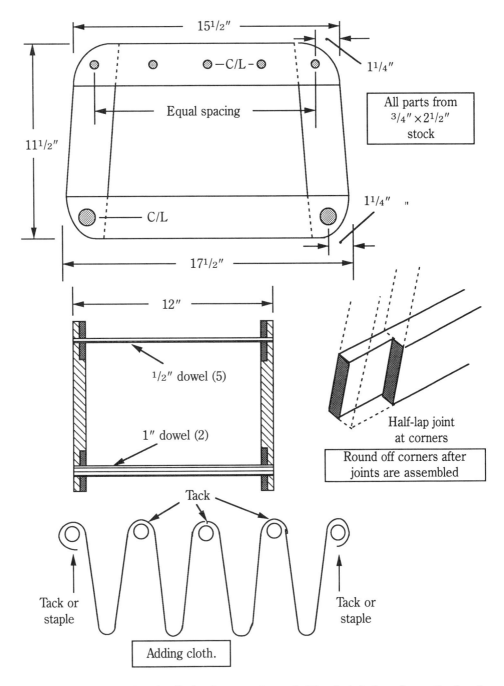

All parts from
$3/4'' \times 2^{1/2}''$
stock

15$^{1}/_{2}$"

1$^{1}/_{4}$"

Equal spacing

11$^{1}/_{2}$"

C/L

1$^{1}/_{4}$"

17$^{1}/_{2}$"

12"

$1/2''$ dowel (5)

1" dowel (2)

Half-lap joint
at corners

Round off corners after
joints are assembled

Tack

Tack or
staple

Tack or
staple

Adding cloth.

Fig. 10-2. *Construction details for the magazine rack. The cloth is draped over the dowels as shown in the lower detail.*

End Table/Mag Rack

The top tray of the project shown in FIG. 10-3 will hold a coffee cup and a little tray of cookies, whereas the bottom tray has ample room for magazines or the daily newspaper. I see it as a kind of personal project, for the individual who wants to be sure that what he or she is reading will be there. The project is light enough so it can be toted to any hiding place. Knotty or clear pine seems right for the project but, as always, there are other options.

Fig. 10-3. The end table includes a small tray at the top and a lower, larger one to hold magazines, newspapers, or books.

The components are assembled as shown in FIG. 10-4; sizes of parts are listed in TABLE 10-1. Start construction by cutting the bottom to size; all other parts can be checked against it to be of precise fitting. Prepare the sides and ends and shape their top edges by following the diagram in FIG. 10-5. Attach the four pieces to the bottom with glue and 6d finishing nails.

Prepare material for the posts (#4) and hold the two pieces together while you make the taper cuts and round off the top edge. Put the posts in place with glue and 4d finishing nails that you drive from inside surfaces.

Put the top tray together as a subassembly, starting with the bottom (#5) and adding the sides and ends with glue and 6d nails. Round off the top ends of the

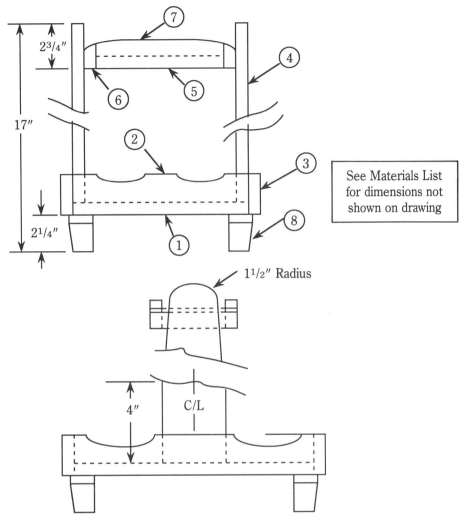

Fig. 10-4. *How the end table/mag rack is put together.*

Table 10-1. Materials List.

Req'd	Part No.	Name	Size
1	1	Bottom	$3/4'' \times 11'' \times 15''$
2	2	Ends	$3/4'' \times 2^{1}/2'' \times 11''$
2	3	Sides	$3/4'' \times 2^{1}/2'' \times 16^{1}/2''$
2	4	Posts	$3/4'' \times 4'' \times 14''$
1	5	Tray bottom	$3/4'' \times 4'' \times 8''$
2	6	Tray ends	$3/4'' \times 1^{1}/2'' \times 5^{1}/2''$
2	7	Tray sides	$3/4'' \times 1^{3}/4'' \times 8''$
4	8	Feet	$1^{1}/2'' \times 1^{1}/2'' \times 2^{1}/4''$

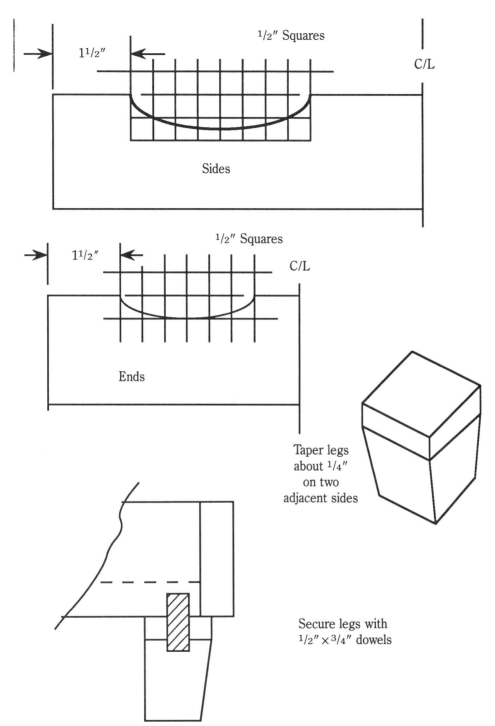

½″ Squares

1½″

C/L

Sides

½″ Squares

1½″

C/L

Ends

Taper legs
about ¼″
on two
adjacent sides

Secure legs with
½″ × ³/₄″ dowels

Fig. 10-5. Details of some of the end table's components.

tray *after* completing the assembly. Coat mating edges of the tray and posts with glue and hold the tray in place with clamps while you drive two 6d finishing nails through the posts.

Shape the feet and attach them to the bottom by using the dowel connection that is shown in FIG. 10-5 or with a single #10 × 1³/₄-inch flat-head screw that you drive through the bottom of the project. The screw can be left exposed but it will be nicer to counterbore the screw hole a bit so the fastener can be concealed with a wooden plug.

Finish naturally or with stain to suit the material you have used. The prototype was toned a light maple and coated with a matte-finish varnish.

Doweled Magazine Rack

The magazine rack in FIG. 10-6 is not a dramatic, new design but it is traditional and a popular home-shop project. Use pine for the ends and the base, and birch or maple dowels. Start work by cutting material for the ends (#1 in TABLE 10-2) to overall size.

Fold a sheet of paper in half and draw a half-profile of the ends by duplicating the shape shown in FIG. 10-7. Cut out the profile with scissors and unfold the paper so you will have a full pattern for marking one of the endpieces.

Hold the two pieces together with doubleface tape so they can be sawed simultaneously. Mark the locations of the ¹/₂-inch holes and drill them before you separate the pieces. Prepare the base and chamfer or, if you prefer, round off its top edges.

Next, cut eleven pieces of ¹/₂-inch dowel, 14 inches long and round off their ends. It will be easier to assemble the dowels and ends now rather than after the base is in place. Coat the insides of the holes with glue before inserting the dowels.

A convenient way to attach the base is to hold it in place temporarily with a few nails that you do not drive in completely, while you drill three holes at each end for #8 × 1³/₄-inch flat-head screws. Remove the nails and after cleaning away waste chips, apply glue to mating areas and install the screws. The screws cannot be seen so leaving them exposed is not objectionable. You can, as is often done

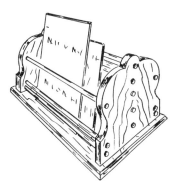

Fig. 10-6. Doweled magazine rack is a classic and popular design.

Table 10-2. Materials List.

Req'd	Part No.	Size
2	1	$^3/_4'' \times 9'' \times 11''$
1	2	$^3/_4'' \times 10'' \times 14''$
11	3	$^1/_2''$ D. $\times 14''$

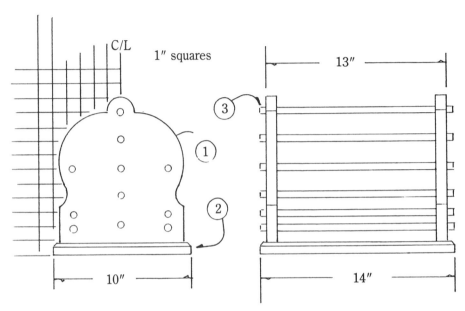

Chamfer edges of base

Round off ends of dowels

Attach base with #8 × 1³/₄" FH screws

Fig. **10-7.** *The doweled magazine rack requires just three components in addition to the dowels.*

on this type of project, finish the bottom with a layer of felt. Self-adhesive felt is available for this purpose, or you can use a spray adhesive to attach a regular felt material.

Wooden Basket

Although the wooden basket is posed containing fruit (FIG. 10-8), it can serve in other capacities—a dry floral display or as a tote for transporting utensils from kitchen to patio. A good way to start construction is to cut the ends to overall size (FIG. 10-9, TABLE 10-3) and join them as a pad for simultaneous shaping. Drill a ¹/₁₆-inch pilot hole for the handle supports before separating the pieces.

Fig. 10-8. *The wooden basket is great for holding fruit but it can serve many other purposes.*

Cut the bottom to size and form a $1/2$-inch-deep-$\times$-$3/4$-inch-wide rabbet at each end. Attach the ends to the bottom with glue and 6d finishing nails.

The fourteen slats that you can provide by making rip cuts on a table saw can be left square or can be treated to conform to one of the shapes suggested in the drawing. If you would like to omit making the slats, check the local lumber yard for a suitable substitute. There are many readymade moldings and trim pieces that are similar or come close in size to what the plan suggests. Attach the slats with glue and a single 3d finishing nail at each end.

Shape the two handle supports and drill the two holes that are required by using the pad-assembly technique. Attach the supports to the basket with #10$\times$ $1^{1}/_{2}$-inch round-head screws. Place a washer under the head of a screw and between the support and the basket.

Cut the handle to length and round off its ends before inserting it in the supports. Use glue at the connections and drive a single 4d finishing nail from the top of the supports into the dowel. Be sure the dowel has been placed so the handle assembly can pivot.

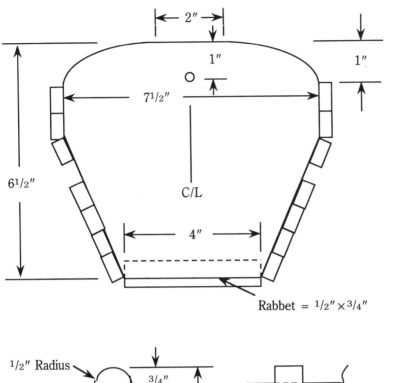

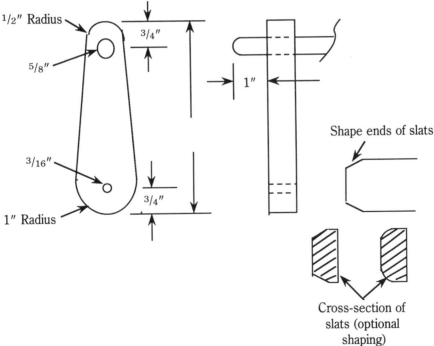

Fig. 10-9. Assembly details of the wooden basket. You can make the slats by ripping on the table saw or substitute a readymade material like slim molding or trim stock.

Table 10-3. Materials List.

Req'd	Name	Size
2	Ends	$3/4'' \times 6 1/2'' \times 7 1/2''$
1	Bottom	$3/4'' \times 4'' \times 12''$
14	Slats	$3/8'' \times 3/4'' \times 13''$
2	Handle support	$3/4'' \times 2'' \times 5 1/2''$
1	Handle	$5/8'' \times 15 3/4''$

The book project was given a coat of sealer and painted white, which seems appropriate, but you might have other ideas. Finishing will be easier if you remove the handle before proceeding.

Bandsawed Baskets

If a bandsaw is part of your shop equipment, you can produce nifty projects like the baskets shown in FIGS. 10-10 and 10-11 with little material and in a surprisingly short time. Limitations, in terms of project size, have to do with the machine. Obviously, a machine with a 6-inch depth-of-cut (not uncommon in a home shop) will handle thicker material than one limited to, say, 4 inches.

For this type of work, the blade must be in prime condition. If it is not sharp, or if it was poorly made so it tends to move off the cut-line, it will be difficult to saw accurately through thick stock. Another factor is that small projects often call for small turning radii so a narrow blade must be used. A slow feed and maximum tension on a $1/8$-inch or $1/4$-inch blade will do much to eliminate bowing. Bowing is a condition that results when the blade, because of dullness, or poor

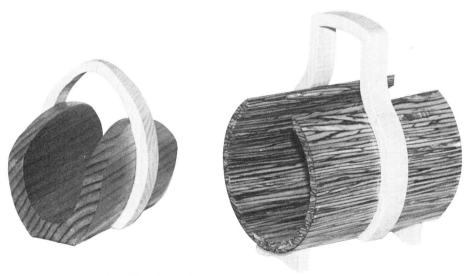

Fig. 10-10. Examples of bandsawed baskets.

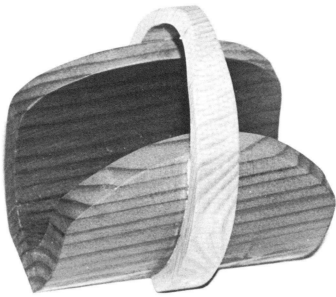

Fig. 10-11. Bandsawed baskets are never very large since the starting block must be selected in relation to the machine's depth of cut.

practice, or even a stubborn grain pattern, arcs in the wood. The result is that the sawed edge is bowed instead of being flat. The possibility of bowing lessens as blade width increases. Often, the condition is slight enough so it can be rectified by sanding or planing.

Any wood can be used so long as you accept that hardwoods like maple and birch and oak will not cut as easily as something like clear pine. Honduras mahogany and walnut are two of the exotic species that are nice to work with. If you think you might like to produce a few of these projects, make the first one of pine, just to get the feel of the procedure.

Figure 10-12 suggests the size of a block to try and shows the step-by-step procedure. The sides are shaped, and the interior is hollowed, with the block held on end. The side profile (step three) is formed with the block's bottom, end down. Often, as is the case with the experiment project, the side profile can be achieved by working on a belt sander, or by hand with a file and sandpaper.

The handle is a fairly straightforward chore—simple cutting of $1/2$-inch or $3/4$-inch stock to a suitable shape and a size that will fit the basket snugly. Since the projects are fairly light, using just glue to attach the handle will provide a connection that is strong enough.

The details for the basket project that is displayed in FIG. 10-13, are shown in FIG. 10-14. Start with a block of wood that is 5 inches square and $5^1/2$ inches long. Use a compass to mark a $4^1/2$-inch circle on one end of the stock and then mark a second, concentric circle to provide a $3/8$-inch wall thickness. Saw on the outside line to provide the basic cylinder and then make the second cut that hollows the inside.

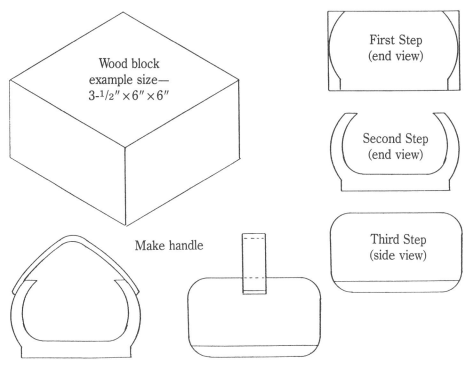

Wood block example size— 3-1/2″ × 6″ × 6″

First Step (end view)

Second Step (end view)

Third Step (side view)

Make handle

Fig. 10-12. The step-by-step procedure that is followed when bandsawing baskets.

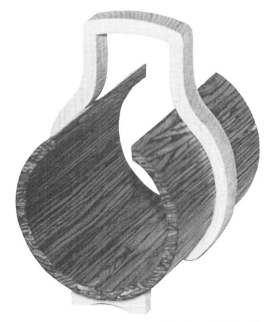

Fig. 10-13. The material used for this bandsawed basket is "Parallam," actually a man-made structural "timber." The grain pattern provides a nice affect.

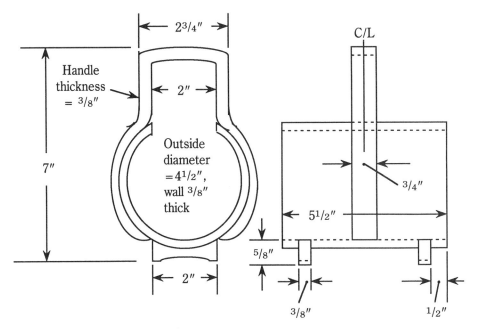

Fig. 10-14. Construction details for the bandsawed basket that was shown in Fig. 10-13.

Make a layout of the handle on a piece of 3/4-inch stock that matches or contrasts with the basket. It's a good idea to use the basket as a template to mark the lower, curved sections of the handle. Cut the handle to shape and sand it smooth before putting it in place with glue. Use 3/8-inch-thick stock for the two feet and add them to the assembly with glue.

Finish the project by applying a first coat of sanding sealer and then several coats of matte-finish varnish.

Bathroom Tissue Caddy

Many households use a crochet stocking to store an extra roll of tissue in the bathroom without its being obtrusive. Our project accomplishes the same purpose but it's a bandsaw project for the woodworker (FIG. 10-15). Start with a block of wood that is about 6 1/4 inches square and 6 inches long. The size of the material dictates that the bandsaw have a 6-inch depth of cut. Although the length of the cylinder that is required for the project does not have to be more than 4 3/4 inches (FIG. 10-16), 6 inches is suggested for the starting block so one sawing operation will produce a cylinder that can be used for both the caddy and the bonus tray that is shown in FIG. 10-17.

Start the project by marking concentric circles on the block; one 6 1/4 inches in diameter, the other 5 1/4 inches. Saw the outside circle and make a slanting entry cut so the inside waste can be removed. Coat the sides of the entry cut with glue

Fig. 10-15. Bathroom tissue caddies are usually like crochet stockings. Ours is a wooden bandsaw project.

and use a band clamp or a piece of slim rope that you twist with a strip of wood to seal the opening. When the glue is dry, slice off $1^{1}/_{8}$ inches of the cylinder. Work on a belt sander or with sandpaper wrapped around a block of wood to true the edges of the parts.

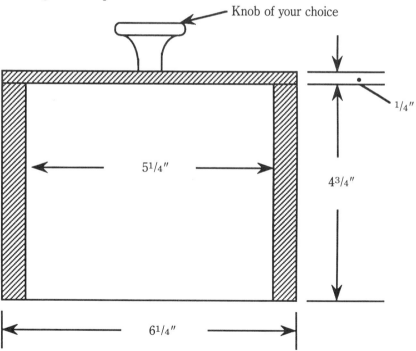

Fig. 10-16. How to make the bathroom tissue caddy. The starting piece was long enough so part of it could be used as a small tray.

Fig. 10-16. Continued.

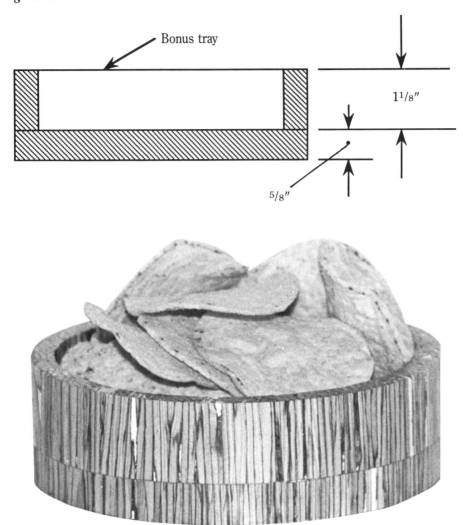

Bonus tray

1¹/₈″

⁵/₈″

Fig. 10-17. The "bonus" tray.

Cut wood for the top of the caddy and the bottom of the tray to a diameter that is a little larger than needed. Put the parts together with glue and keep them united with clamps or by using weights. When the glue is dry, the added components can be sanded to conform to the contour of the cylinders.

Lots of finishing options depend on the wood that was used and the decor of the bathroom. Use a natural finish for a modern look or, for a homespun appearance, use paint and decorate with decals.

Turned Vase

The project on display in FIG. 10-18 shows how you can make projects like vases and bowls that seem to have been produced on a lathe. The idea is to preform rings or other shapes with centered holes and assemble them with glue (FIG. 10-19).

Fig. 10-18. *The small vase looks like a lathe turning but is actually a set of wooden rings that were glued together.*

The easiest way to form the openings is with hole saws or a fly cutter in a drill press. Do not cut the pieces to size before you form the holes or they will not be large enough to clamp safely when you are cutting the holes. Instead, make a layout of the holes on a large piece of stock and cut out sections after the hole-forming operation. Rings can be cut when power tools are lacking by working with a coping saw as shown in FIG. 10-20.

Projects of this type can be simple or they can appear more complex. As shown in FIG. 10-21, much depends on the attention you give perimeters before you do the assembly. Even elementary forms can be "fancied" by special finishing treatments. A Fleck Stone finish is interesting and since the material supplies excellent coverage, it reduces the amount of final sanding that must be done.

Another textured finish you can try, one that was used on the project in FIG. 10-18, is to coat the item with a product called Durham's water putty. It comes dry,

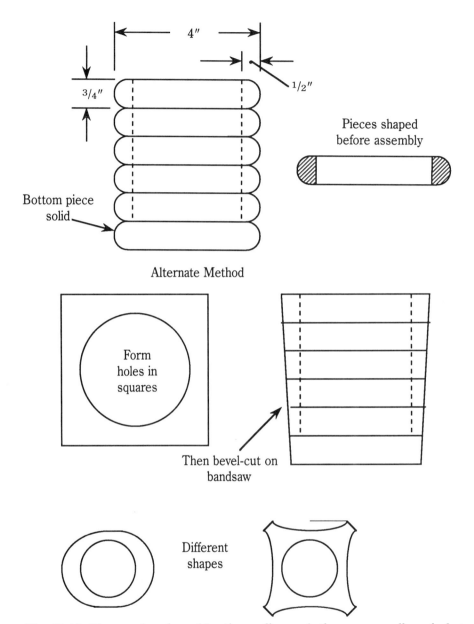

4"

3/4"

1/2"

Pieces shaped
before assembly

Bottom piece
solid

Alternate Method

Form
holes in
squares

Then bevel-cut on
bandsaw

Different
shapes

Fig. 10-19. The procedure for making the small vases is the same regardless of what outside shape you decide on.

as a white powder that is mixed with water. Its normal function is as a patching or molding material but a fluid mixture can be applied by brush. The consistency of the mix (how much water is used) will determine the texture of the application. The water putty can be finished in various ways after it is completely dry.

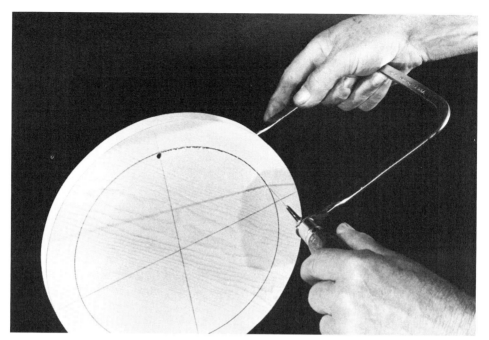

Fig. 10-20. *Rings can be cut by using a coping saw. An entry hole allows passing the blade through the work before it is installed in the frame.*

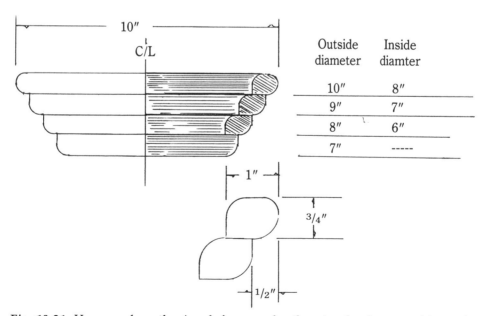

	Outside diameter	Inside diamter
	10″	8″
	9″	7″
	8″	6″
	7″	-----

Fig. 10-21. *How you shape the rings before you glue them together has everything to do with the appearance of the project.*

Table Lamp

The base for the table lamp (FIG. 10-22) is a solid block of wood that is kerfed to receive contrasting strips for an inlaid effect. One of the problems with making wooden bases is forming the center hole for the lamp cord. This is easily solved if a suitable extension bit is available. In this case, start with a block that is 5

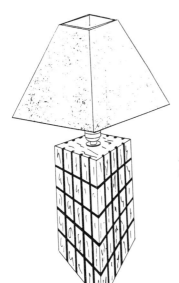

Fig. 10-22. The base for the table lamp is a solid block that is kerfed to receive contrasting strips of wood.

inches × 5 inches × 10 inches. An alternate method is offered in FIG. 10-23. Provide two pieces 2¹/₂ inches × 5 inches × 10 inches and after forming a ¹/₂-inch-wide-×-¹/₄-inch-deep dado down the center of each one, glue them together to form a solid block. Next, form saw kerfs about ³/₁₆ inch deep parallel to the long dimension, with 1-inch spacing. A normal saw kerf is ¹/₈ inch so the contrasting strips should measure ¹/₈-inch-thick × ¹/₄-inch-wide × a little more than 10 inches long. Coat one edge of the strips with glue and then tap them into place in the kerfs. Use a pad or belt sander to sand the strips flush after the glue has set.

Next, form the crosskerfs, spacing them 2 inches. Provide contrasting strips and install them by following the procedure that was outlined earlier.

The installation method for the electrical parts is shown in FIG. 10-24. Counterbore a 1-inch hole about ¹/₂ inch deep in the base of the project and drill a ¹/₄-inch hole through one side to meet with the counterbore. The pipe, washers, nuts, and socket are standard items that are available in home-supply centers. Secure the pipe with washers and nuts at both ends and thread through the electrical cord. Form a loose knot in the cord where it passes through the counterbore. Attach the base of the socket by threading it on the pipe and securing the lock screw. The final step is to wire the socket and press it into place.

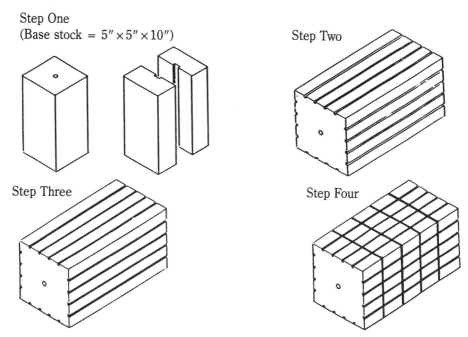

Step One
(Base stock = 5″×5″×10″)

Step Two

Step Three

Step Four

Fig. 10-23. *Use a solid block of wood for the lamp base if you have an extension drill that is long enough to form the center hole.*

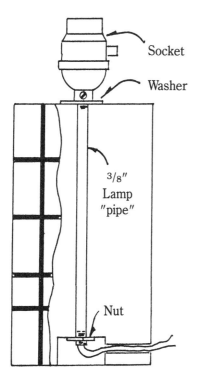

Socket

Washer

³/₈″
Lamp
"pipe"

Nut

Fig. 10-24. *How the electrical components for the table lamp are installed.*

Two Cases for Playing Cards

Having special storage cases for a deck or two of playing cards is a good way to keep them in prime condition. Those that are tossed about soon have ragged edges and lose their rigidity. Two designs are offered here (FIGS. 10-25, 10-26). Ours are made of birch with mahogany trim but other species would be just as suitable; cherry and birch, or maple and mahogany, for example.

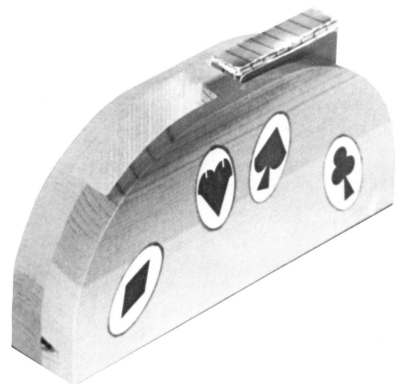

Fig. 10-25. Card case #1 has slots for two decks of cards.

Both of the projects are started by making two of the component that is shown in FIG. 10-27. The voids, which are essentially wide dadoes, can easily be cut on a table saw or radial-arm saw. They can also be formed using the hand-tool technique that was described in chapter 1. Another way to work is to glue 1/2-inch and 1-inch-wide- × -3/8-inch-thick strips of wood to a 3/8 inch-thick base.

For case #1 (FIG. 10-28), glue the two primary parts together and add a 1/4-inch-thick bottom. Cut the bottom oversize so it can be sanded flush after the glue has set. Remove the bulk of the waste at the top corners by sawing, and use sandpaper to smooth the edges.

Fig. 10-26. Card case #2 will also hold two decks of cards but it is designed like a small chest.

Card cases require two of these parts

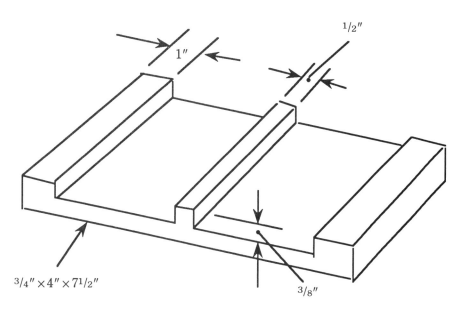

Fig. 10-27. Both of the card cases require two of these components.

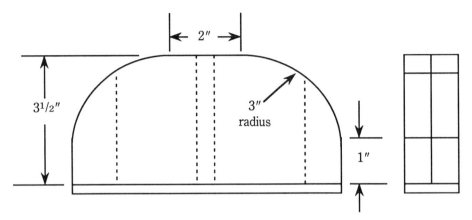

2″

3¹/₂″

3″
radius

1″

Fig. 10-28. Card case #1. Assemble all the parts before you shape the top edge.

For case #2 (FIG. 10-29), close in the basic parts by adding ¹/₄-inch-thick sides. Don't round off the corners until you have drilled the holes and installed the dowel in the bottom section. Do the corner rounding with top and bottom sections held together.

It seems appropriate for projects like this to have a natural, satiny-smooth finish. Perform an initial sanding and apply a coat of sanding sealer. Sand again, and after applying a couple of coats of varnish, rub all surfaces glass smooth with fine steel wool. Be sure the final application of varnish is bone dry before you work with the steel wool.

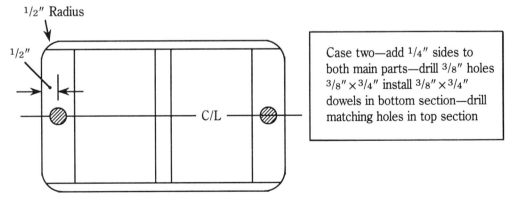

¹/₂″ Radius

¹/₂″

C/L

Case two—add ¹/₄″ sides to both main parts—drill ³/₈″ holes ³/₈″ × ³/₄″ install ³/₈″ × ³/₄″ dowels in bottom section—drill matching holes in top section

Fig. 10-29. Card case #2. Be very accurate when you drill the top and bottom units for the dowel.

Pen/Pencil Holder

Pens and pencils are everywhere but not one is at hand. The answer lies in making the project shown in FIG. 10-30 so an assortment of writing implements will always be readily available.

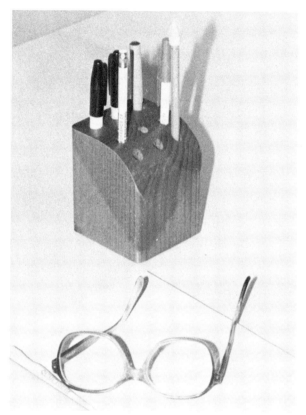

Fig. 10-30. A quickee project that will hold pens and pencils close at hand.

Start with a block of hardwood that measures 3 1/2 inches square × 4 inches long with the grain pattern running the long dimension. Mark the locations of the 3/8-inch and 1/2-inch holes (FIG. 10-31) and drill all of them 3 inches deep. When you drill holes this deep, retract the bit frequently to clear away waste chips. This provides for a cleaner hole and less buildup of heat that can burn the wood or the cutting tool.

Use a saw to form the top/front corner and sand it smooth. Round off the four corners of the project and use fine sandpaper to smooth all surfaces and edges. A coat or two of sealer followed by waxing is about all the finish the project requires.

A final touch would be to cut small circles of thin foam rubber and to bottom them in the holes so the tips of pens and pencils will not be marred when they are dropped into place.

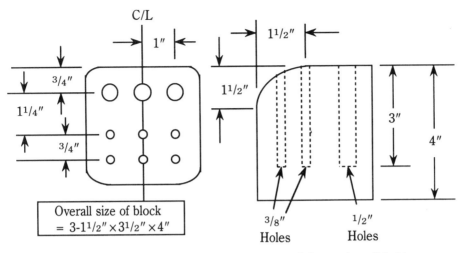

C/L

1″

1¹/₂″

³/₄″

1¹/₄″

³/₄″

1¹/₂″

1¹/₂″

3″

4″

Overall size of block
= 3-1¹/₂″ × 3¹/₂″ × 4″

³/₈″
Holes

¹/₂″
Holes

Fig. 10-31. Drill all the holes before you shape the top of the pen/pencil holder.

Bud Vase

Bud vases, like the example on display in FIG. 10-32, are quick lathe projects that are welcome holders for pretty flowers. They are suitable for dried flowers when the center hole is left as-is, but will serve for live flowers if the hole is sized to suit a small test tube for holding water.

Fig. 10-32. The bud vase is a quick lathe-project. If you plan on showing live flowers, drill the hole to accommodate a small test tube.

The stock, preferably a hardwood, is mounted on a small faceplate for turning. The hole can be formed while the wood is in the lathe by using the common lathe technique of mounting a chuck in the tailstock of the machine. An alternate method is to remove the work after it is turned and to drill the hole on a drill press.

Figure 10-33 offers two designs for duplicating but do not feel limited. Little variations are certainly permissible or you can just go your own way. For those

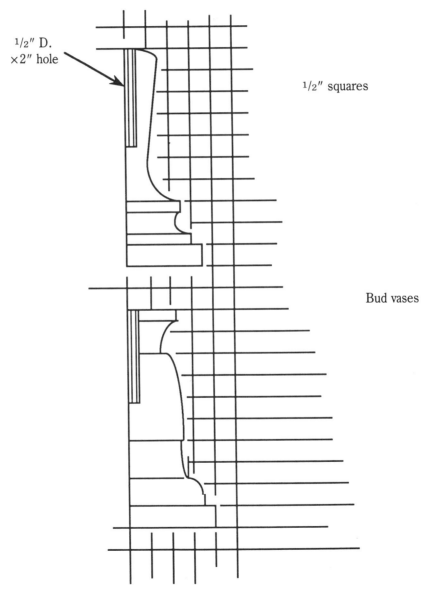

1/2" D. ×2" hole

1/2" squares

Bud vases

Fig. 10-33. Two designs for bud vases.

who do not own a lathe, check out the readymade wooden spindles that are available at lumber yards and home-supply centers. Many of these have sections that can be cut out and used as bud vases. The only other chore required is to drill the center hole.

A Case for Pennies

If you are like me, and many other folks, you have a jar or some other container in which you drop pennies when you empty your pockets. It's fun to accumulate them (for some reason) but there is the chore of counting so they can be traded for paper money. Thinking like a grandparent, I thought of crating the coins and presenting the wealth to a youngster (FIG. 10-34). No more counting, and little Joe had fun.

Fig. 10-34. It's even more fun to watch a child open the penny crate than it is to make it.

The crate should be simple, something along the lines suggested in FIG. 10-35, held together with just small nails so it can be easily opened. To eliminate the counting frustration, include the measuring gadget that has troughs to hold fifty pennies. To make it, follow the details that are shown in FIG. 10-35. Slice the block

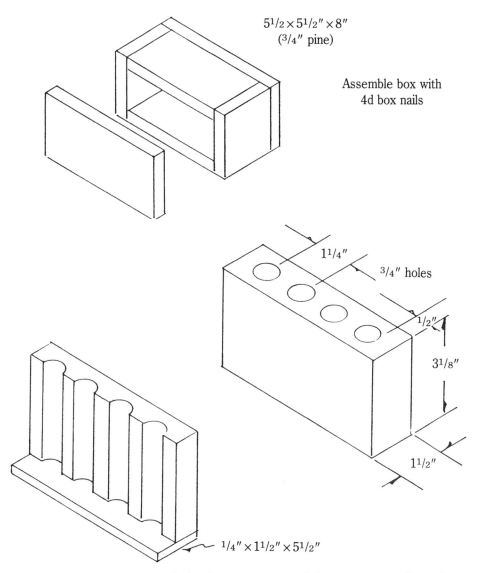

5$^1/_2$ × 5$^1/_2$" × 8"
(3/4" pine)

Assemble box with
4d box nails

1$^1/_4$"

3/4" holes

$^1/_2$"

3$^1/_8$"

1$^1/_2$"

$^1/_4$" × 1$^1/_2$" × 5$^1/_2$"

Fig. 10-35. Construction details for the penny crate and the penny-measuring gadget.

apart on its centerline after the holes are drilled and mount a section on a $^1/_4$-inch-thick base. When you slice the block, favor one side of the centerline so the troughs will be full semicircles.

The project doesn't require, in fact should not have, a fancy finish. Just sand it smooth and then use a felt-tip pen to mark it like the one in FIG. 10-36.

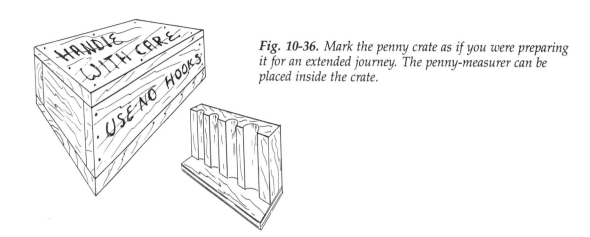

Fig. 10-36. Mark the penny crate as if you were preparing it for an extended journey. The penny-measurer can be placed inside the crate.

Treasure Chest

A gift for milady? Sure, but no sex bias here. The project shown in FIG. 10-37 will adapt for use by male or female. Maple, birch, walnut, and mahogany are all good choices for the material. There are other options, more exotic species like

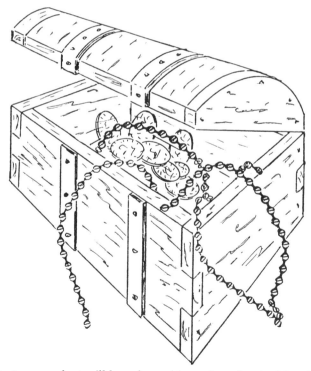

Fig. 10-37. The treasure chest will be welcomed by male or female. Line the inside of the chest with gold-colored felt.

teak or cocabola or rosewood that suit the concept, but whatever, choose a hardwood.

The drawing in FIG. 10-38 shows how the project is assembled; TABLE 10-4 lists the sizes of the parts that are needed. Start by cutting the ends and the sides (#1 and 2) to overall size. Hold the two sides together with doubleface tape and lay out the shape of the tongue. Since the pad is only 1 inch thick, the sawing can easily be done on a scroll saw or by hand. If you work by hand, use a backsaw or a dovetail saw. Next, make a pad of the two endpieces and form the notch to fit the tongue on the sides. Work carefully to produce a precise connection between ends and sides. Hold the four pieces together with clamps after coating mating areas with glue.

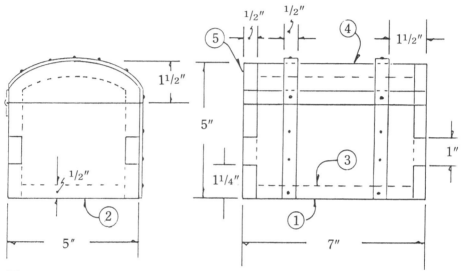

Fig. 10-38. How the treasure chest is put together.

Table 10-4. Materials List.

Req'd	Part No.	Size
2	1	$1/2'' \times 31/2'' \times 7''$
2	2	$1/2'' \times 31/2'' \times 5''$
1	3	$1/2'' \times 4'' \times 6''$
1	4	$11/2'' \times 5'' \times 6''$
2	5	$1/2'' \times 11/2'' \times 5''$

Cut the bottom (#3) to size, checking against the box assembly to be sure of an accurate fit. Add the bottom by using just glue and clamps.

Cut the piece for the major part of the lid (#4) and check FIG. 10-39 to see how the part may be shaped. You can duplicate the half-profile by using tracing paper or simply make your own layout on the end of the component. The more kerfs

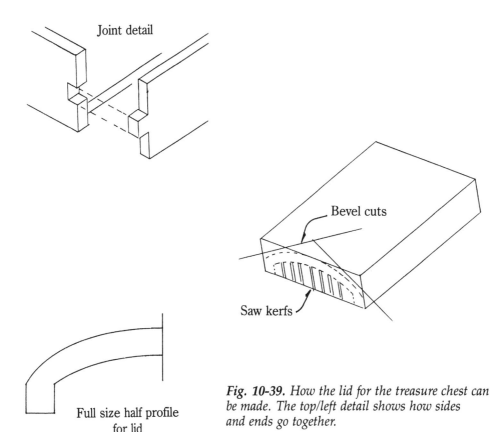

Joint detail

Bevel cuts

Saw kerfs

Full size half profile
for lid

Fig. 10-39. *How the lid for the treasure chest can be made. The top/left detail shows how sides and ends go together.*

you cut the easier it will be to remove the waste with a chisel, but saw carefully since the depth of the cuts must vary to suit the inside contour of the lid.

Shape the top contour by first making bevel cuts to remove the bulk of the waste, and finish the job on a belt sander or by using a file and sandpaper. Cut the ends (#5) to size and attach them to the lid by gluing and clamping. Shape the ends to conform to the contour of the lid after they have been attached. Check the lid assembly against the body of the chest and do some sanding, if necessary, to be sure it fits correctly.

Before going further, be sure the assemblies are thoroughly sanded and finished. A natural finish seems in order regardless of the material you have chosen. Apply a coat of sanding sealer and after you have smoothed it with fine sandpaper, apply a couple of coats of matte-finish varnish, sanding between applications and after the final one. The finish should be smooth and sans gloss.

There are many designs in small, brass hinges that you can use to connect lid to body, or you can opt for $1/4$-foot or $1/2$-inch piano hinge that you cut to a suitable length. The decorative straps for the chest are provided by cutting $1/2$-inch-wide strips of sheet brass. Attach the strips with 1/2-inch-long, brass escutcheon pins. It's not essential that the straps be made of brass. Use aluminum or copper if you feel the metal will combine better with the wood species you've chosen.

Candle Sconce

The candle sconces (FIG. 10-40), while emulating light sources that were in use at one time, are not intended to provide illumination in the modern home, but they can contribute a romantic atmosphere, or just be part of a wall decor even if the candles are never lit.

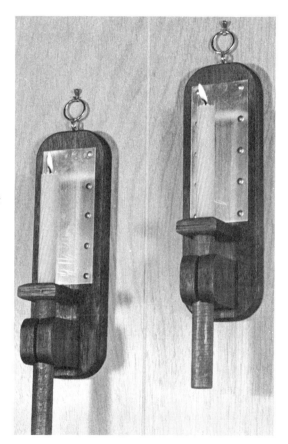

Fig. 10-40. The candle sconces won't provide much illumination but they can be more romantic than electricity.

Cut the back to size (FIG. 10-41) and round off its corners. Provide the aluminum reflector and attach it to the back with 1/2-inch escutcheon pins. Cut the post holder to size and drill the hole for the post. The hole must be slightly undersize so the post will be held wherever it is positioned. Use a backsaw or dovetail saw to form the kerf. Attach the holder to the back with glue and a single #8 × 1³/4-inch flat-head screw.

Cut the candle platform to size and drill the blind hole for the post. Drill a small hole through the platform for the 4d box nail and put the nail in place before gluing post and platform together. The nail is there so candles can be impaled on it. An alternate method is to attach a small candle cup to the platform.

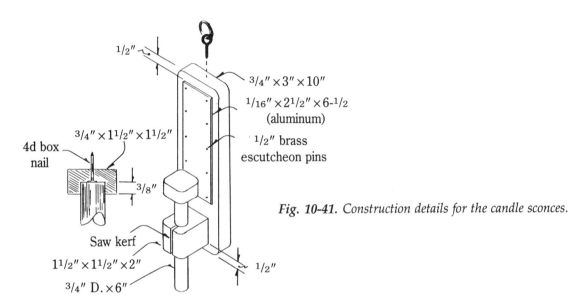

1/2"

3/4" × 3" × 10"

1/16" × 2¹/2" × 6-¹/2
(aluminum)

3/4" × 1¹/2" × 1¹/2"

4d box
nail

¹/2" brass
escutcheon pins

3/8"

Fig. 10-41. *Construction details for the candle sconces.*

Saw kerf

1¹/2" × 1¹/2" × 2"

3/4" D. × 6"

1/2"

Flower Pot Holder

The flower pot holder serves a practical purpose and provides a whimsical touch if it is decorated as shown in FIG. 10-42. There are many times when a plant is brought home in a common clay pot. The project allows displaying the plant while concealing its prosaic container. The arrangement can be permanent. The book project is made of pine and painted white but, as always, you can choose a different material and a preferred finish.

Start by cutting a piece of 3/4-inch-×-6¹/2-inch-×-8-inch stock for the bottom and two pieces 3/4 inch × 5⁵/8 inches × 6¹/2 inches for the sides (FIG. 10-43). Form the rabbets in the bottom and assemble sides and bottom with glue and 4d box nails that you drive up through the bottom.

Cut two pieces of 3/4-inch-×-10-inch-×-10-inch stock for the ends and join them as a pad. Fold a sheet of paper in half and draw half of the profile of the end. Use scissors to cut on the lines you have drawn and then unfold the paper so you will have a full plan for the component. Attach the plan to the wood with a spray adhesive or just use it as a template to mark the wood.

Fig. 10-42. The whimsical flower pot holder. You don't have to duplicate the scowl. Draw your own picture or use decals.

After the parts are sawn to shape, attach them to the subassembly with glue and 6d finishing nails that you set and conceal with wood dough. You can decorate whimsically as we did or leave the project plain or apply some suitable decals.

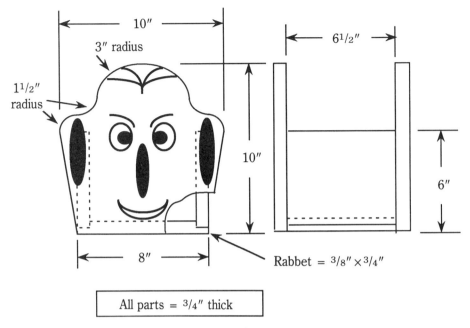

Fig. 10-43. How the flower pot holder is made.

All parts = 3/4" thick

3" radius

1½" radius

10"

10"

8"

6½"

6"

Rabbet = 3/8" × 3/4"

Utility Stool

The utility stool is a "use when needed" project although when not used as a seat for a child or a footstool for a grownup, it can serve to display a plant or some other object (FIG. 10-44). The project can be made of shop-grade plywood but if it is not going to be hidden when it is idle, why not use a cabinet-grade, lumber-core plywood.

The legs are two 3/4-inch-×-12-inch-×-12-inch pieces (FIG. 10-45). Hold them together as a pad and make the layout for the relief area. The top 2-inch radius can be shaped by using a fly cutter in the drill press to form a 4-inch hole. Straight cuts complete the job. This is not a bad procedure to use since the fly cutter produces a disc that can be stored for use on some other project. Of course, making a full saw cut on scroll saw or bandsaw will also get the job done.

Form the notches for the cross-lap joint. Make two parallel saw cuts 3/4 inch apart and 3 inches long and clean away the waste with a chisel or by making repeat, overlapping saw cuts. Do the work carefully so the parts will mesh snugly but without having to be forced, and so their top edges will be on the same plane.

Draw a 13-inch circle on the plywood and saw out the disc. Attach the disc to the legs with glue and 6d finishing nails. Set the nails and conceal them with wood dough before you do final sanding and finishing.

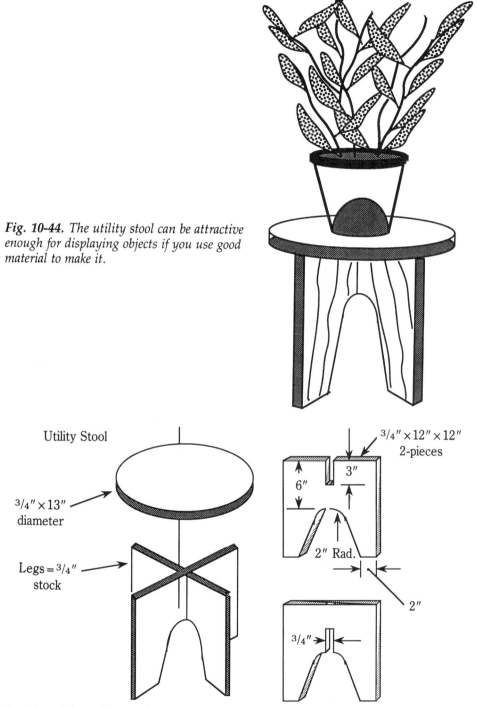

Fig. 10-44. *The utility stool can be attractive enough for displaying objects if you use good material to make it.*

Utility Stool

$3/4'' \times 13''$
diameter

Legs = $3/4''$
stock

$3/4'' \times 12'' \times 12''$
2-pieces

3''

6''

2'' Rad.

2''

$3/4''$

Fig. 10-45. *The utility stool requires these three pieces. Saw carefully when forming the notches for the cross-lap joint. The legs should go together snugly without being forced.*

Tie/Scarf Rack

The tie/scarf rack folds neatly against a wall so it uses minimum storage space but its arm can be raised so the items it holds can easily be removed (FIGS. 10-46, 10-47, 10-48).

Start the project by sawing a piece of 3/4-inch-×-3½-inch-×-8-inch stock to the shape shown in FIG. 10-49. Make the 3/4-inch-×-1³/8-inch-×-3½-inch riser block and attach it to the back with glue and 4d nails. Drive the nails from the back so they cannot be seen.

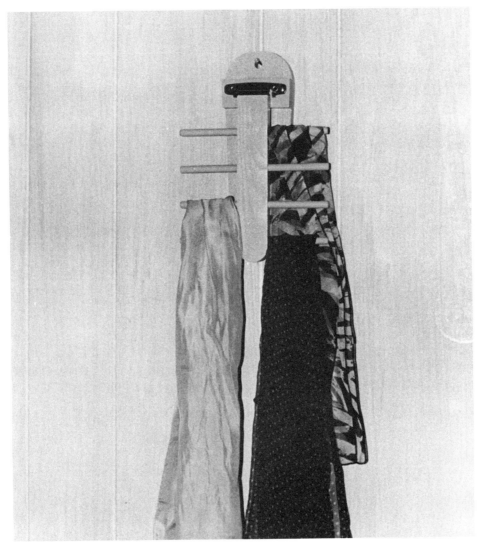

Fig. 10-46. The tie rack uses little space since it folds against the wall.

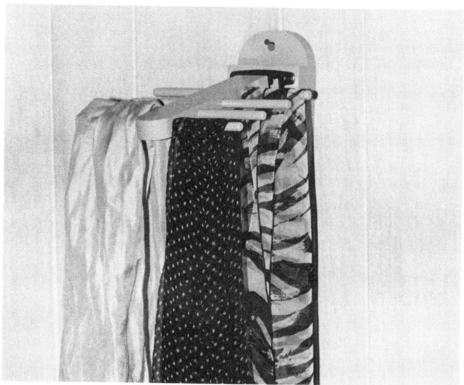

Fig. 10-47. Extending the arm allows easy access to the stored items.

Fig. 10-48. The self closing hinge will keep the arm extended if light items like ties and scarfs are stored. It won't work for items like heavy belts.

Cut the arm to size and, after rounding off the end, drill the four holes for the 3/8-inch dowels. Cut the dowels to length and round off or chamfer their ends. Install the dowels after coating the inner surfaces of the holes in the arm with glue. Drive two 5/8-inch brads from the back of the arm into each of the dowels.

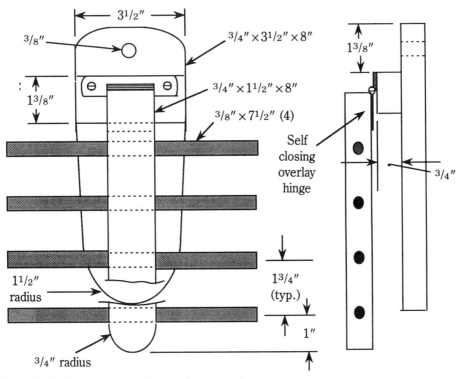

Fig. 10-49. *How the tie rack is made.*

Attach the arm to the riser block with a self closing overlay hinge. The hinge is a standard item, normally used on cabinet doors, that can be found in any respectable hardware store. The spring action of the hinge is strong enough to hold the arm extended so long as you don't overload it. Ties, scarfs, and kerchiefs are okay, but not items like heavy belts.

Whorlwinds

Whorlwinds (a name I created for the projects) are fun to make and watch, and I can tell you from experience that they make most welcome gifts. They are charming as contemporary decorative accents in or out of the house and when they are correctly suspended, the spiral shapes will rotate in the slightest movement of air, providing constant changes of motion. When they are given a glossy finish, clear, or paint, reflected light moves vertically from slat to slat, up or down, depending on the direction of rotation of the project.

There is no one specific design for whorlwinds even though the construction procedure does not vary regardless of the final shape. Trying to preview during the initial stages what the results will be, may or may not work, but it does not matter. If the product does not please you it can be redone quickly and without wasting material. Some typical whorlwinds are displayed in FIGS. 10-50, 10-51, and 10-52.

Fig. 10-50. *Whorlwinds provide delightful garden accents. When suspended correctly they will rotate in the slightest breeze.*

Fig. 10-51. The shapes of whorlwinds are limited only by your imagination.

The projects are an assembly of similar strips of wood that are mounted on a threaded rod and held tightly together by nuts on the ends of the rod. There are many options of wood species that can be used, but whatever the choice, the material must be dry, smooth, and flat so each strip (or slat) will bear solidly against its neighbor. A softwood like pine, hardwoods like maple, and birch are good choices. There might be enough of a particular wood species in the scrap bin for a project or two. Readymade materials like lattice strips and slight-trim strips that are available in lumber yards are other options. Experiment.

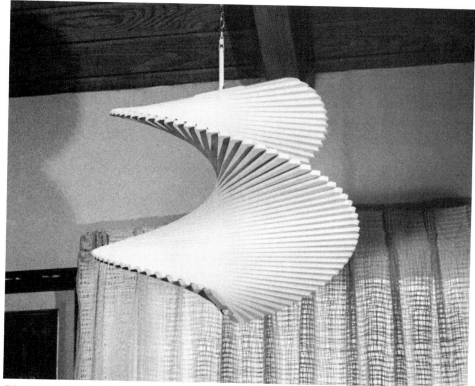

Fig. 10-52. *Whorlwinds are also at home indoors. This one, rather heavy, hangs from small chain.*

If you rip the strips from base stock, use a hollow ground, or a carbide-tipped planer blade so sawed edges will be smooth. The length of the strips is arbitrary but their thickness should be in the 1/4-inch to 3/8-inch range; their width, from 1/2 inch to 3/4 inch. Generally, the longer the strips, the thicker and wider they can be.

The next step after the strips are prepared is to drill the mounting hole. This must be done accurately so make the jig that is shown in FIG. 10-53. Use one drilled strip as a template, placing it on top of the stack that is in the jig. The same jig can be used for strips of different length or thickness, but you will need another jig if you make strips of different width.

After the holes are drilled, thread the strips on a piece of threaded rod that is about 2 inches longer than the stack. Use a small washer and a lock nut on the bottom of the rod and a washer and plain nut at the top. Tighten the nut just enough to hold the strips firmly together, place the assembly on a flat surface and use a pad or belt sander to smooth both surfaces.

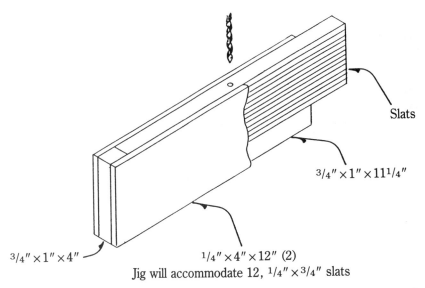

Slats

$3/4'' \times 1'' \times 11^{1}/4''$

$3/4'' \times 1'' \times 4''$ $1/4'' \times 4'' \times 12''$ (2)

Jig will accommodate 12, $1/4'' \times 3/4''$ slats

Fig. 10-53. A jig you can make so the slats for whorlwinds can be drilled accurately.

Mark the stack for the profile cuts. This is the point where you try to visualize what the project will look like when the strips are spread. Some ideas that you can try are shown in FIG. 10-54. There is a lot of leeway here, and once you have finished the first project, you will recognize the possibilities for original designs.

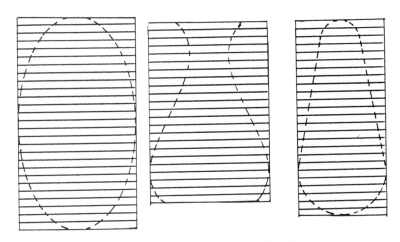

Fig. 10-54. The final shape of whorlwinds is determined by the profile you cut when the stack of strips is flat. You will be in a better position to preview results after you have made one or two.

Fig. 10-54. Continued.

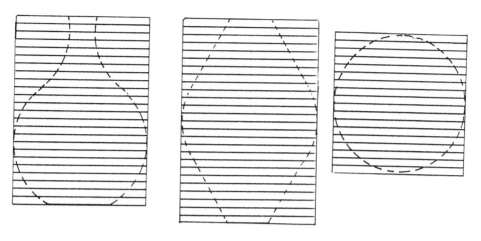

Saw the profile on a scroll saw, bandsaw, saber saw, or by hand with a cop-ing saw and smooth the sawed edges. The project will be more interesting if you shape the ends of the strips while the assembly is still flat. Any of the forms that are shown in FIG. 10-55 can be adopted. If you have a shaper or a portable router you can think about forming an interesting contour.

Fig. 10-55. Shaping the ends of the slats when they are stacked flat will add more interest to the projects.

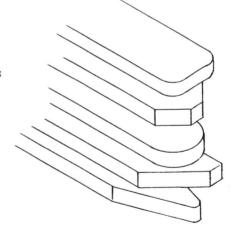

After sanding and shaping has been accomplished, grip the bottom end of the rod in a vise and turn each strip the same number of degrees. Be sure the strips are tight enough on the rod so they will hold their places. When all strips are positioned, tighten the top nut just enough to ensure that the strips will stay where they were placed. Over tightening may cause the strips to bow.

There are many ways to suspend the whorlwinds. The first step is to supply a finial along the lines of those suggested in FIG. 10-56. The electrical terminal can be secured to the rod by squeezing it with a pair of pliers. If you use tubing, select it with a small enough inside diameter so it can be tapped to fit the rod. A lamp finial might be usable even if you have to retap the hole.

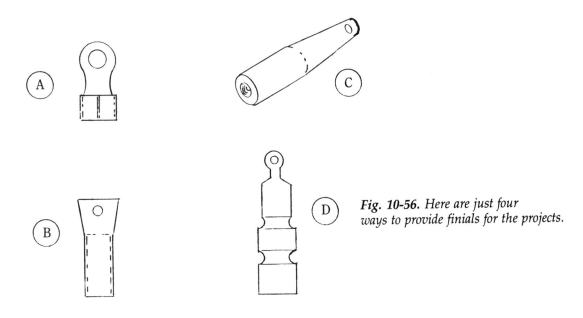

Fig. 10-56. Here are just four ways to provide finials for the projects.

A. Electrical terminal
B. Tubing—flattened and drilled
C. Custom-made from steel rod
D. Readymade lamp finial

The projects will turn nicely if you hang them with strong fishing line and a ball-bearing fishing-line swivel (FIG. 10-57). The swivels, and the line will be available in a sporting goods store and, often, in the outdoors section of department stores.

Use a sealer on the projects to begin with whether you decide on a natural or painted finish. Final coat should be a glossy varnish or enamel. Finishing is best done with a spray type can of paint. Be sure to read the instructions on the container, especially those that apply to safe use.

If you would like to depart from the usual method of hanging the whorlwinds, check the idea that is shown in FIG. 10-58. The project is mounted on a ball bearing that has an inside diameter that suits the rod. The bearing is press fitted in a counterbored hole formed in a round or square base.

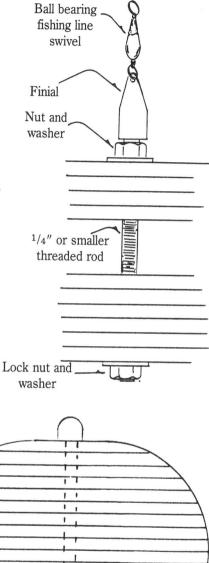

Ball bearing
fishing line
swivel

Finial

Nut and
washer

Fig. 10-57. *Using fish-line swivels will ensure that the projects will rotate easily.*

1/4" or smaller
threaded rod

Lock nut and
washer

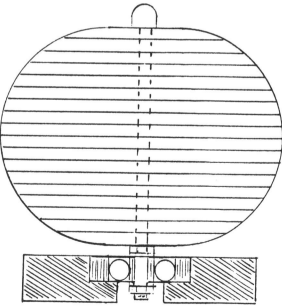

Fig. 10-58. *This is one way to make a table-top whorlwind. The project rotates on a ball bearing that is press-fitted in the base.*

Garden Shrine

Shrines occupy a niche in many gardens, sometimes projecting a religious ambience, other times just contributing to the general scene. Regardless of what they display, they lend an air of peace and quiet to a special garden area. The one shown in FIG. 10-59 incorporates a container for colorful flowers that add to the projects appeal.

Fig. 10-59. A shrine is an ever popular project for the garden. It can hang on a wall, like this, or on a post that's set in the ground.

Construction details and material requirements are offered in FIG. 10-60 and TABLE 10-5. Because a decidedly outdoor, worn look seemed appropriate, we decided to work with rough, 2-inch and 1-inch redwood.

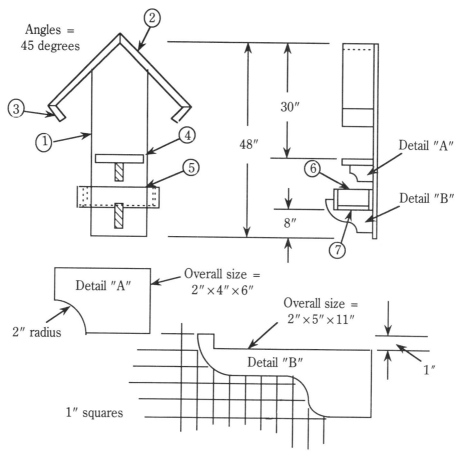

Fig. 10-60. Construction details for the shrine. Rough redwood is a suitable material.

Table 10-5. Materials List.

Req'd	Part No.	Size
1	1	$2'' \times 14'' \times 48''$
2	2	$2'' \times 8'' \times 21''$
2	3	$2'' \times 6'' \times 8''$
1	4	$2'' \times 8'' \times 10''$
2	5	$3/4'' \times 5'' \times 20''$
2	6	$3/4'' \times 4 1/4'' \times 8 1/2''$
1	7	$3/4'' \times 8 1/2'' \times 20''$

Start the project by forming the back (#1). Since the part is 14 inches wide, it will have to be made by edge-gluing two pieces 7 inches wide. The 45-degree angle cuts at the top can be made before or after the parts are joined. Cut parts for the shelter (#2 and 3) and make 45-degree miter cuts on the ends that will be joined. Put these parts together as a subassembly using waterproof glue and 5d galvanized nails. Add the shelter to the back with glue and 16d nails.

Next, make the supports for the shelf and the container, first cutting them to overall size and shaping them to the contours that are shown as details A and B in FIG. 10-60. Attach the supports to the back with glue and 16d nails.

Cut all the parts that are required for the container and put them together using glue and 7d nails at all connections. Drill about four 1/2-inch holes through the bottom for drainage before installing the unit. Coat all mating areas with glue. Drive 6d nails through the bottom into the support; 7d nails through the rear of the container into the back of the project.

The last construction step is to make the shelf and to install it with glue and 16d nails. Drive nails through the shelf into the support and from the rear of the project into the back edge of the shelf.

We did some distressing on the project, using a rasp and coarse sandpaper to give edges a worn look, and denting some surfaces with light hammer blows. An appropriate way to finish the shrine is to allow it to weather for awhile and to give it several applications of an exterior-type sealer. The project can be attached to a wall or to a post that is set in the ground.

Rural Mailbox

If you live in an area where mail is delivered at the road you might enjoy making the cover that is shown in FIG. 10-61. The project provides good support and ample protection for a large mailbox and what will be delivered to it. The design is essentially a rigid frame (FIG. 10-62) that is covered with standard redwood or cedar roof shakes. Use waterproof glue and galvanized nails at all connections. Study the assembly details in FIG. 10-63 and the material requirements in TABLE 10-6 before starting construction.

Begin by making the frame for the roof. Cut parts #1 and the triangular gusset (#6). Cut 45-degree miters at one end of parts #1 and join them with the gussets, using glue and 5d nails. The two subassemblies are joined with the five crosspieces (#2). Here, use 12d box nails.

Next, make parts #3 and 4. These will be U-shaped when assembled, with the top ends of the vertical pieces (#3) mitered to conform with the slope of the roof frame. These subassemblies are connected to the roof frame with parts #7. The drawing shows a particular shape for these components but it is not something you must adhere to. What is important is that the angular cut matches the pitch of the roof. Make the connections with glue and 6d box nails. The final step

Fig. 10-61. The rural mailbox.

for the frame is to cut the platform for the mailbox (#5) and to install it with glue and 9d nails.

Add the shakes by starting at the lower edge of the roof frame. The second layer of shakes can overlap the first one a considerable amount. Attach the covers with 4d nails that you drive into the roof-frame members. Be sure the joints of the shakes are staggered and that the top ones cover the joints of the lower ones. Make the ridge as shown in detail A and put it in place with glue and a few 6d nails. The mailbox is secured to the platform as shown in detail B.

Figures 10-64 and 10-65 show how the project can be attached to a post and how the post should be installed in the ground. The post hole doesn't have to be more than 6 inches in diameter. The less ground you disturb the stronger the installation will be.

There are standards to follow when locating the mailbox. These have to do with the height of the box and its distance from the road (FIG. 10-66). The standards, which can be supplied by the local post office, are necessary so delivery can be convenient for the carrier.

Fig. 10-62. *The rural mailbox project is essentially a frame that is covered with standard roof shakes.*

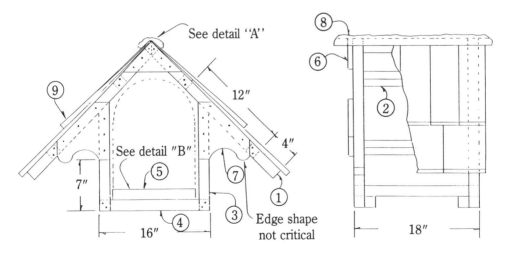

Fig. 10-63. *How the rural mailbox goes together. It looks more complicated than it really is.*

Fig. 10-63. Continued.

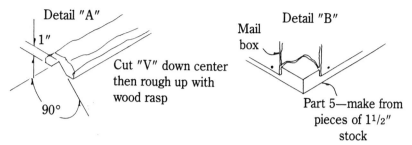

Detail "A"

1"

90°

Cut "V" down center
then rough up with
wood rasp

Detail "B"

Mail
box

Part 5—make from
pieces of 1¹/₂"
stock

Table 10-6. Materials List.

Req'd	Part No.	Size	Material
4	1	1¹/₂″ × 1¹/₂″ × 27″	Redwood
5	2	1¹/₂″ × 1¹/₂″ × 15″	″
4	3	1¹/₂″ × 1¹/₂″ × 15″	″
2	4	1¹/₂″ × 1¹/₂″ × 16″	″
1	5	1¹/₂″ × 12″ × 18″	″
2	6	³/₄″ × 4″ × 8¹/₂″	″
4	7	³/₄″ × 8″ × 8″	″
1	8	1¹/₂″ × 3¹/₂″ × 22″	″
Enough to cover about 12 square feet	9		Cedar or redwood shakes

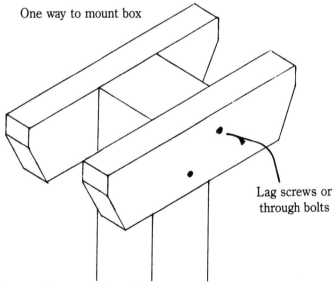

One way to mount box

Lag screws or
through bolts

Fig. 10-64. One way to mount the mailbox on a post.

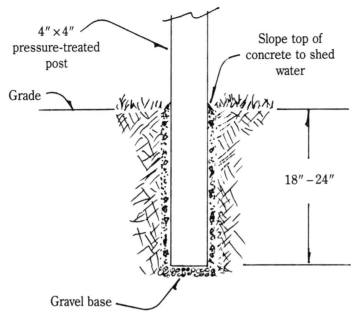

Fig. 10-65. *The professional way to set a post in the ground.*

4" × 4"
pressure-treated
post

Slope top of
concrete to shed
water

Grade

18" – 24"

Gravel base

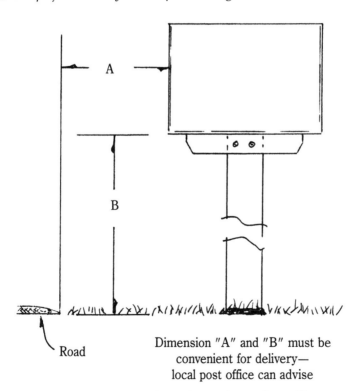

Fig. 10-66. *The local post office will tell you how to locate the mailbox.*

A

B

Road

Dimension "A" and "B" must be
convenient for delivery—
local post office can advise

Sawhorse

The sawhorse ranks high on any list of convenience accessories you can make for use in and out of the shop. Use them to support work to be sawed, as scaffolding and as temporary workbenches when they are spanned with boards or plywood. Those shown in FIG. 10-67 are designed for rigidity and a long life. Figure 10-68 shows the components in assembled form; material requirements are listed in TABLE 10-7.

Start by providing pieces for the legs (#2) and marking the shape that is required on one of them. After sawing it to shape, use it as a pattern to mark the others. If you have a bandsaw, you pad two, maybe the four pieces, depending on the capacity of the machine, and saw them simultaneously. Next, provide the beam (#1) and join legs and beam with glue and 1/4-inch-×-4-inch lag screws. Drill pilot holes for the screws before you drive them.

Cut the braces (#3 and 4) oversize, as suggested, and add them to the assembly with glue and 7d nails. Saw off the ends of the braces so they will conform to the slant of the legs.

Figure 10-67 shows one sawhorse with a lower shelf. The shelf is a wise addition since it adds stability and provides some storage area for tools in use. If you

Fig. 10-67. Sawhorses are woodworker's best friend in or out of the shop.

add it, place the lower braces on the inside of the legs so they can provide a ledge for the shelf. A shelf of 3/4-inch exterior-grade plywood put in place with glue and 6d nails will work.

Finish the project with several applications of sealer. Some workers cover the beam of the sawhorse with a strip of carpeting.

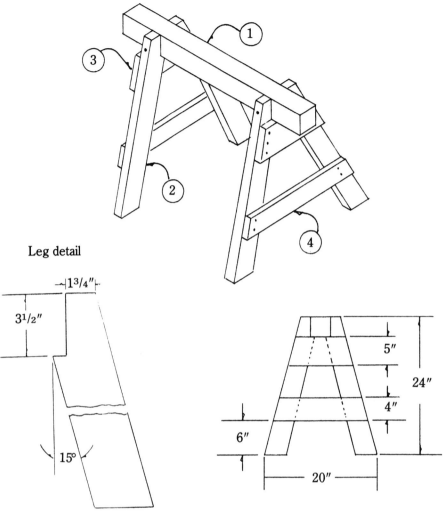

Leg detail

‒|1³/₄″|‒

3¹/₂″

15°

5″

24″

4″

6″

20″

Attach legs to beam with ¹/₄″ ×4″ lag screws braces to legs with 7d nails

Fig. 10-68. *How to put together a sturdy, long-lived sawhorse.*

Table 10-7. Materials List.

Req'd	Part No.	Size
1	1	3¹/₂″ × 3¹/₂″ × 36″
4	2	1¹/₂″ × 3¹/₂″ × 27″ (oversize)
2	3	³/₄″ × 5″ × 14″ (oversize)
2	4	³/₄″ × 4″ × 20″ (oversize)

Dowel Storage Rack

The problem of storing the supply of dowels that are nice to have on hand is solved by making the storage unit that is shown in FIG. 10-69. It provides for dowels of different diameters and includes a drawer for related items like readymade dowel pins, shaker pegs, and so on. Figure 10-70 shows the various components and how they are assembled; TABLE 10-8 lists the sizes of the parts.

Start with the sides, cutting material to overall size and holding the pieces together as you saw the tapers that reduce the width of one end to 6 inches. Make the bottom and the lower shelf (#2 and 3) and assemble them and the sides with glue and 4d box nails.

Cut the upper shelves (#4 and 5) to size and hold them together as shown in the drawing detail. Working this way allows the holes that are needed for the dowels to be drilled in both shelves simultaneously and ensures that the holes will have true, vertical alignment. Put the drilled shelves in place with glue and 4d nails through the sides of the project.

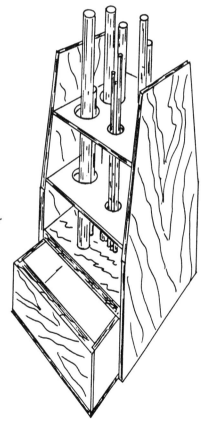

Fig. 10-69. The dowel rack includes a drawer for accessory items.

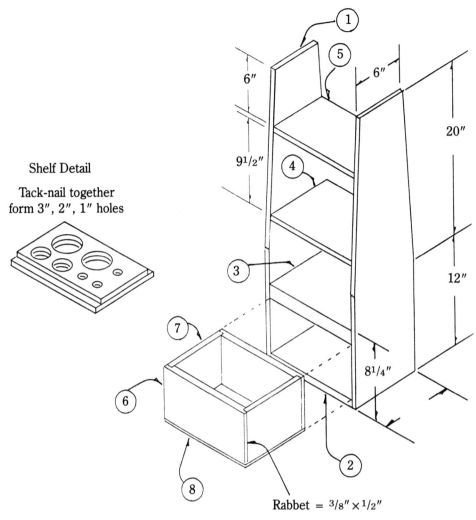

Shelf Detail

Tack-nail together
form 3", 2", 1" holes

6"

6"

9¹/₂"

20"

12"

8¹/₄"

Rabbet = ³/₈" × ¹/₂"

Attach sides to shelves with 4d nails
drawer bottom with 3d
other parts with 3d
(use glue all joints)

Fig. 10-70. *Assembly details for the dowel rack. The drawer isn't fancy but it's practical.*

The drawer is not fancy but it serves the purpose. Cut all the parts that are required but before forming the rabbets in the front and the back, check the sizes of the pieces against the assembly to be sure the drawer will slide easily. Attach front and back to the sides with glue and 3d finishing nails, and add the bottom, using glue in the connection and securing with 3d finishing nails. Use sandpaper

Table 10-8. Materials List.

Req'd	Part No.	Size
2	1	$1/2'' \times 8'' \times 2''$
1	2	$3/4'' \times 8'' \times 11''$
1	3	$1^1/2'' \times 8'' \times 11''$
1	4	$1/2'' \times 7^1/2'' \times 11''$
1	5	$1/2'' \times 6^1/2'' \times 11''$
2	6	$3/4'' \times 5^3/4'' \times 11''$
2	7	$1/2'' \times 5^3/4'' \times 7^1/4''$
1	8	$1/4'' \times 8'' \times 11''$

to round off the bottom edges of the drawer. The handle for the drawer can be a plain block of wood or a readymade knob.

Finishing is optional but it would seem that for a shop accessory, a good sanding followed by several applications of sealer is the best way.

Index

Other Bestsellers of Related Interest

ONE-WEEKEND COUNTRY FURNITURE PROJECTS
—*Percy W. Blandford*

Transform simple materials into beautiful, functional objects with its brand-new selection of original projects to use in and around your home, in an easy, one-weekend format, especially for time-conscious hobbyists. A basic understanding of woodworking techniques is all you need to build an attractive, durable piece of furniture in as little as 12 hours. You get nearly 50 original project plans—all requiring only simple hand tools and inexpensive materials—and ample drawings and instructions for every design. 24-pages, 163 illustrations. **Book No. 3702, $14.95 paperback, $24.95 hardcover.**

CLOCKMAKING:
18 Antique Designs for the Woodworker
—*John A. Nelson*

Create timepieces of everlasting beauty and service using this illustrated, step-by-step guide to building antique clock reproductions. From the elegant long-case Grandfather clock to the one-of-a-kind Banjo clock, there is something here for woodworkers of all tastes and skill levels. Nelson's instructional savvy takes you through cutting the pieces, assembling the parts, and preparing, distressing, and finishing the wood to achieve an authentic look. 240 pages, 136 illustrations. **Book No. 3164, $18.95 paperback, $26.95 hardcover.**

MAKING POTPOURRI, COLOGNES AND SOAPS: 102 Natural Recipes
—*David A. Webb*

Fill your home with the scents of spring—all year long! This down-to-earth guide reintroduces the almost forgotten art of home crafts. You'll learn how to use simple ingredients (flowers, fruits, spices, and herbs) to make a variety of useful scented products, from soaps and deodorant to potpourris and colognes. Webb demystifies this age-old craft and offers step-by-step diagrams, work-in-progress photographs, and easy-to-follow recipes to give you everything you need to create your own home crafts. 144 pages, 98 illustrations. **Book No. 2918, $9.96 paperback, $18.95 hardcover.**

KATHY LAMANCUSA'S GUIDE TO FLORAL DESIGN
—*Kathy Lamancusa, C.P.D.*

Create exquisite silk and dried floral designs for every room of your home with this easy-to-follow guide. You'll learn to work with the various materials and supplies and master basic design techniques quickly and easily with step-by-step photographs and instructions. Then you'll go beyond the legendary baskets, and special occasion designs. 128 pages, 166 illustrations. **Book No. 3491, $12.95 paperback, $21.95 hardcover.**

KATHY LAMANCUSA'S GUIDE TO WREATH MAKING
—*Kathy Lamancusa, C.P.D.*

Now, you can enjoy the inviting charm of handcrafted wreaths in your home all year long. Lamancusa clearly explains the most intricate aspects of wreath making. Beginning with the basics, you'll look at the materials used in wreath making with instructions for locating, cutting, and combining them. Then you'll move on to such projects as bows, kitchen wreaths, seasonal wreaths, wreaths for children, romantic wreaths, masculine wreaths, special occasion wreaths. 128 pages, 133 illustrations. **Book No. 3492, $10.95 paperback, $19.95 hardcover.**

COUNTRY CLASSICS:
25 Early American Projects
—*Gloria Saberin*

If you like to work with wood, you can easily make authentic reproductions of Early American antiques by following the plans in this guide. Each project, selected for its unique charm and simplicity, includes a photo of the finished piece, historical information about the item, materials list, instructions, working plans, and construction tips. A special section of full-color photographs is also included. 184 pages, 198 illustrations. **Book No. 3587, $12.95 paperback, $19.95 hardcover.**

STENCILING MADE EASY
—Wanda Shipman

Easy-to-use supplies and materials have renewed the versatile and creative art of stenciling in home design. This book provides illustrated instruction that shows how you can simply, economically, and attractively use stenciling to brighten walls, floors, wood, tinware, fabric, and paper. Important guidelines in choosing colors and designs to complement the style and decor of your home are also included. 128 pages. Illustrations. **Book No. 3167, $14.95 paperback only.**

REFINISHING OLD FURNITURE
—George Wagoner

This is the place to look for answers on how to choose the proper finish, make simple repairs, select the best refinishing methods, and care for and touch up your projects. The easy-to-use format includes illustrations, a summary of materials and applications, safety guidelines, addresses for material suppliers, a glossary of refinishing terms, and a list of other helpful books. 192 pages, 96 illustrations. **Book No. 3496, $12.95 paperback, $19.95 hardcover.**

Prices Subject to Change Without Notice.